QUICK QUILTS
FROM YOUR
SCRAP BAG

EDITED BY

PATRICIA WILENS

Oxmoor
House®

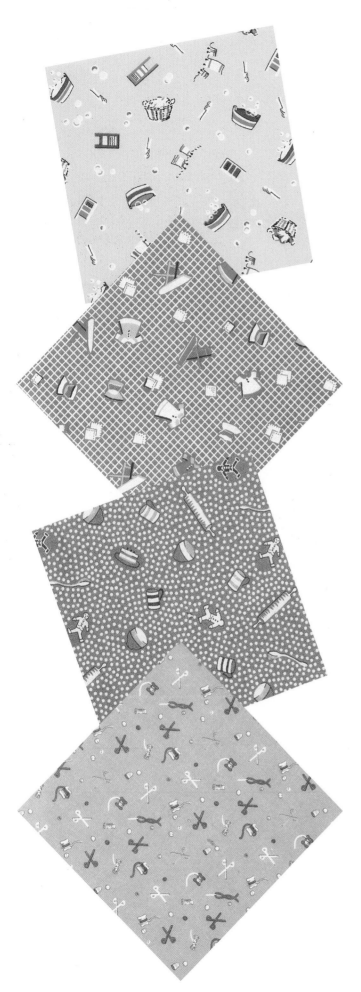

Quick Quilts from Your Scrap Bag
from the *For the Love of Quilting* series
©1999 by Oxmoor House, Inc.
Book Division of Southern Progress Corporation
P.O. Box 2463, Birmingham, Alabama 35201

Published by Oxmoor House, Inc. and Leisure Arts, Inc.

Library of Congress Catalog Card Number: 99-70342
Hardcover ISBN: 0-8487-1906-9
Softcover ISBN: 0-8487-1907-7
Printed in the United States of America
First Printing 1999

Editor-in-Chief: Nancy Fitzpatrick Wyatt
Senior Crafts Editor: Susan Ramey Cleveland
Senior Editor, Copy and Homes: Olivia Kindig Wells
Art Director: James Boone

Quick Quilts from Your Scrap Bag
Editor: Patricia Wilens
Contributing Copy Editor: Susan S. Cheatham
Contributing Designer: Carol O. Loria
Illustrator: Kelly Davis
Senior Photographer: John O'Hagan
Photo Stylist: Linda Baltzell Wright
Director, Production and Distribution: Phillip Lee
Associate Production Manager: James McDaniel
Production Assistant: Faye Porter Bonner

We're Here for You!

We at Oxmoor House are dedicated to serving you with reliable information that expands your imagination and enriches your life. We welcome your comments and suggestions. Please write to us at:

Oxmoor House, Inc.
Scrap Quilts Editor
2100 Lakeshore Drive
Birmingham, AL 35209

To order additional publications, call 1-205-877-6560.

FOR THE LOVE OF FABRIC

What is this love affair that quilters have with fabric? We usually say that piecing is our favorite part, or hand quilting. But I'm convinced that most of us make quilts simply because we *love* fabric—the texture, color, and feel of it is utterly enchanting.

For me, the love of fabric started young. I passed many a rainy afternoon rummaging through a cedar chest that held the remnants of my grandmother's career as a milliner. I spent hours playing with velvets, satins, and laces, imagining myself a princess decked out for the ball.

Today, I make scrap quilts. I am considered a very organized person (okay, some people think I'm compulsive), but there's something about the riotous jumble of a scrap quilt that warms my heart. A scrap quilt has an exuberant energy that a more sedate quilt cannot imitate.

The charm lies in all the different fabrics—pretty prints cheek by jowl with cheery plaids, an exotic batik nestled against a somber solid. Making a scrap quilt is theoretically frugal, using up leftovers from past projects. The truth is, a scrap quilt is a wonderful excuse to own more fabric. My friend Marti Michell puts it this way—"a scrap is any piece of fabric I haven't used yet," even if it's a 3-yard length.

The best way to make a scrap quilt is to just let it happen. If you try to coordinate, the quilt won't have the spontaneity that invigorates a successful scrap quilt. To keep yourself in check, put ready-to-sew scraps in a pillowcase. (Use three pillowcases to sort light, medium, and dark values.) Pull out any scrap your hand touches. Vow to use the fabric you pull out, no matter what. You'll put fabrics together that you'd never pair in any other situation—that's part of the fun.

Please enjoy the up-to-date quick-piecing methods and step-by-step instructions in this book, whether your quilt is traditional or hip-hop. Most of all, have a good time playing with your fabrics.

Patricia Wilens

Editor

TABLE OF CONTENTS

SUMMER BASKETS

Quilt by Tracey M. Brookshier of Capitola, California; machine-quilted by Laura Lee Fritz of Napa, California

Tracey Brookshier likes bold, bright, way-out-there, in-your-face *color*.

"My favorite part of quilting is choosing all the fabrics to go into a quilt," Tracey says, "and my favorite quilts have lots of different fabrics."

The fabrics in *Summer Baskets* all coordinate with the colors in the sumptuous border fabric, which appears as a unifying element in the center of each basket.

Finished Size
Quilt: 85¾" x 100"
Blocks: 50 (10" x 10")

Materials
2¾ yards print border fabric
1½ yards coordinating fabric (lime) for setting triangles
⅜ yard inner border fabric
50 (7" x 13") basket fabrics*
49 (6" x 21") tone-on-tone prints for block backgrounds*
1 yard binding fabric
2⅝ yards 108"-wide backing
*Note: You can substitute 17 fat quarters for baskets and another 17 fat quarters for block backgrounds.

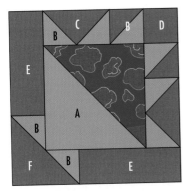

Basket Block—Make 50.

Cutting

Instructions are for rotary cutting and quick piecing. For traditional cutting and piecing, use patterns below and on pages 10 and 11. Cut all strips cross-grain except as noted.

From border fabric
- 4 (6¾" x 90") lengthwise strips for outer border.
- 25 (6⅞") squares. Cut each square in half diagonally to get 50 A triangles.

From setting fabric
- 5 (15½") squares. Cut each square in quarters diagonally to get 18 setting triangles (and 2 extra).
- 2 (8") squares. Cut each square in half diagonally to get 4 corner triangles.

From each basket fabric
- 1 (6⅞") square. Cut square in half to get 1 A triangle. Discard extra triangle or use for another block.
- 2 (2⅞") squares. Cut 1 square in half to get 2 B triangles. Save second square for triangle-squares.
- 4 (2½") squares for B piecing.

From binding fabric
- 1 (32") square for bias binding. Add remainder to block background fabrics.

From each background fabric
- 1 (5") square. Cut square in half diagonally to get 1 F triangle. Discard extra triangle or use for another block.
- 1 (2⅞") square for B triangle-squares.
- 2 (2½" x 6½") E pieces.
- 2 (2½" x 4½") C pieces.
- 1 (2½") D square.

Block Assembly

1. For each block, select a set of A and B basket pieces, a set of B, C, D, E, and F background pieces, and 1 border print A triangle (Block Assembly Diagram). Join A triangles; press seam allowances toward basket fabric.

2. Lightly mark a diagonal line on wrong side of 1 (2⅞") B square of basket fabric. Match this with same-size square of background fabric, right sides facing. Stitch ¼" seam on both sides of line (Diagram A). Press. Cut apart on drawn line to get 2 B triangle-squares.

3. See page 11 for instructions on diagonal-corners technique. Use this method to sew 2½" squares to corners of each C rectangle (Diagram B).

4. Sew B triangles to ends of each E piece, making sure triangles point in opposite directions as shown.

5. Lay out units (Block Assembly Diagram). Join B triangle-square to end of B/C unit at top of block. Sew combined unit to top edge of A square.

6. Join D, B triangle-square, and B/C unit. Sew combined unit to right side of block.

7. Sew B/E strips to left and bottom edges as shown. Then sew F triangle to bottom left corner to complete block. Make 50 blocks.

continued

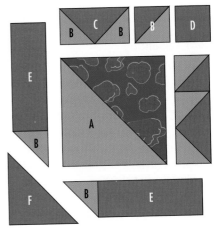

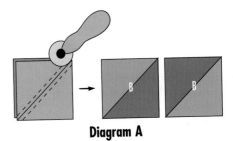

Block Assembly Diagram

Diagram A

Diagram B

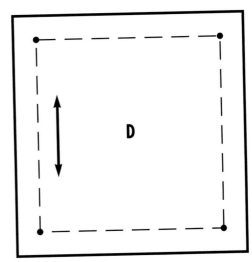

D

Quilt Assembly

1. Lay out blocks in 10 diagonal rows (Quilt Assembly Diagram). End rows with setting triangles as shown. Move blocks around to achieve a nice balance of color and fabrics. When satisfied with block placement, join blocks and triangles in each row.
2. Join rows to complete quilt center. Sew corner triangles in place as shown.

Borders

1. Cut 8 (1½"-wide) strips of inner border fabric. Sew 2 strips end-to-end for each border.
2. Measure length of quilt through center of quilt top. Trim 2 border strips to match length. Sew these to quilt sides, easing to fit as needed. Press seam allowances toward borders. Repeat for top and bottom borders.
3. Add outer border strips in same manner.

Quilting and Finishing

1. Mark quilting design on quilt top as desired. Quilt shown is outline-quilted by machine with free-motion quilting (with red thread) adding hearts and curlicues around each basket.
2. Layer backing, batting, and quilt top. Baste. Quilt as desired.
3. Use remaining binding fabric to make 10½ yards of continuous straight-grain or bias binding. Bind quilt edges.

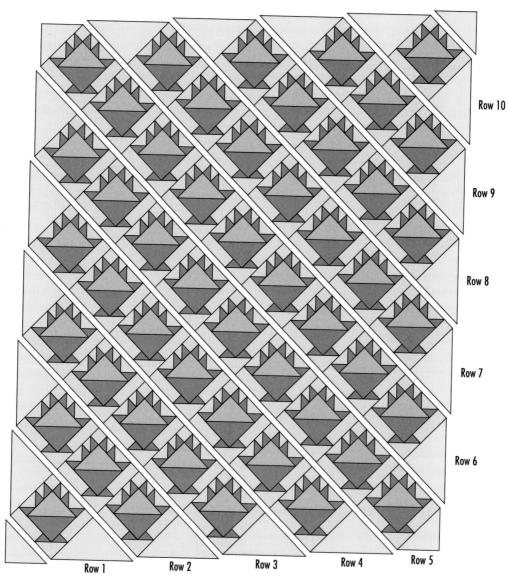

Row 10

Row 9

Row 8

Row 7

Row 6

Row 1   Row 2   Row 3   Row 4   Row 5

Quilt Assembly Diagram

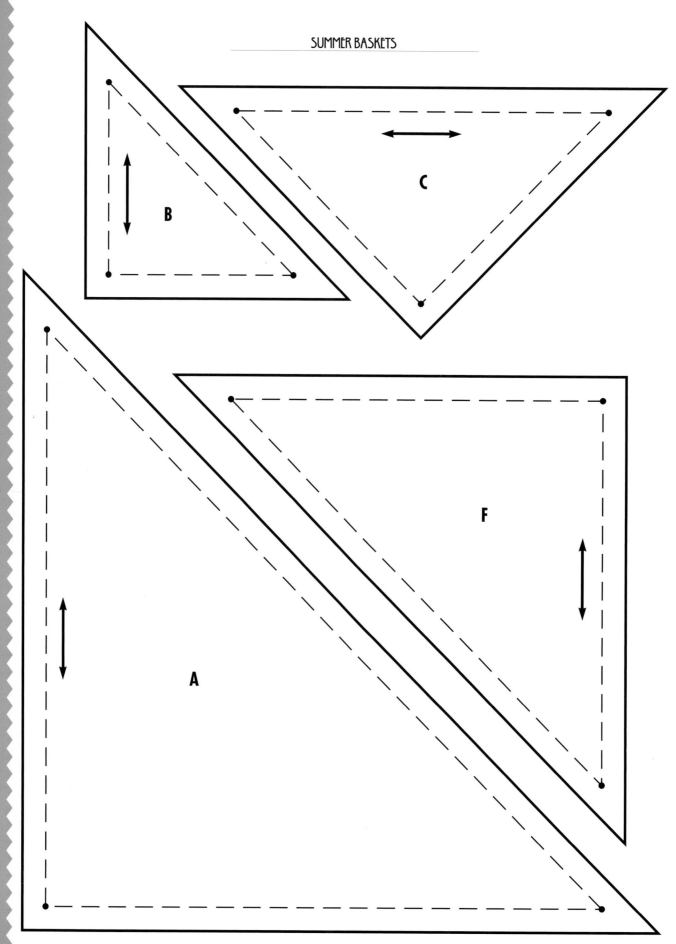

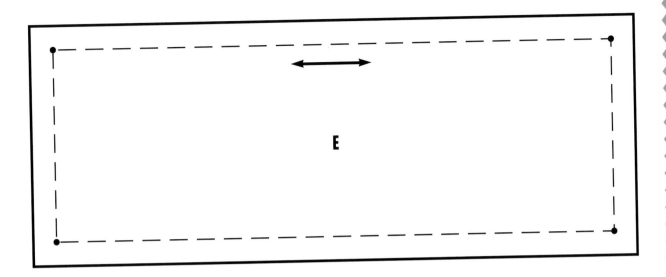

E

DIAGONAL-CORNERS QUICK-PIECING METHOD

The diagonal-corners technique turns squares into sewn triangles with just a stitch and a snip. This method is particularly helpful if the corner triangle is very small, because it's easier to handle a square than a small triangle. And, by sewing squares to squares, you don't have to guess where seam allowances match, which can be difficult with triangles.

1. A seam guide will help you sew diagonal lines without having to mark the fabric. Draw a line on graph paper. Place paper strip on throatplate; lower needle onto line. (Remove foot if necessary for a good view.) Use a ruler to verify that line is parallel to needle. Tape paper in place; then trim paper as needed to clear needle and feed dogs.

2. Match small corner square to corner of base fabric, right sides facing. Align top tip of small square with needle and bottom tip with seam guide (Photo A). Stitch from tip to tip, keeping bottom tip of small square in line with seam guide.

3. Press corner square in half at seam (Photo B).

4. Trim seam allowance to ¼" (Photo C). Repeat procedure as needed to add a diagonal corner to 2, 3, or 4 corners of base fabric.

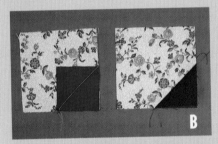

VINTAGE SCOTTIES

Quilt by Sonja Palmer of Plymouth, Minnesota

Scottish terriers were very popular during Franklin D. Roosevelt's presidency, thanks to well-known presidential pet, Fala. A gift from a cousin, Fala came to the White House in 1940. He greeted many visiting dignitaries and traveled with FDR around the world. You can use real feedsack material for this quilt, or choose reproduction prints.

Finished Size
Quilt: 17¾" x 21¼"
Blocks: 15 (3¼" x 4¼")

Materials
19 (3½" x 4½") scraps for appliqué
4 (2") squares for ball stripes
⅛ yard *each* 4 prints for borders
½ yard muslin
⅛ yard *each* 2 binding fabrics
1 (21" x 25") rectangle for backing
Black embroidery floss
Paper-backed fusible web (optional)

Cutting

Measurements include ¼" seam allowances, except for appliqué pieces. For hand appliqué, add a scant seam allowance. If fusing, fuse web to wrong side of fabric following manufacturer's instructions and cut out shapes finished size.

From assorted prints
• 15 Scotties.
• 4 balls.

From 2" squares
• 4 ball stripes.

From each of 2 border fabrics
• 1 (1¼"-wide) strip.

From each remaining border fabric
• 1 (1½"-wide) strip for borders.

From muslin
• 2 (3¾"-wide) strips. From these, cut 15 (3¾" x 4¾") rectangles for appliqué background.
• 1 (3"-wide) strip. From this, cut 4 (3") squares for border corners.
• 2 (1¼"-wide) strips for borders.

From each binding fabric
• 2 (2" x 23") strips.

Block Assembly

1. Hand-appliqué a Scottie to each muslin rectangle, using 2 strands of floss for blanket-stitch. Or fuse Scotties in place; then add blanket-stitch. Add a French knot for each dog's eye. (See Stitch Diagrams below.)
2. Appliqué a stripe onto each ball. In quilt shown, ball stripes were appliquéd using traditional appliqué with matching thread.
3. Blanket-stitch each ball onto a muslin square.

Quilt Assembly

1. Referring to photo, join Scottie blocks into 5 horizontal rows of 3 blocks each. Join rows.
2. Join 1 wide and 1 narrow border strip to sides of a muslin border strip to make a strip set. Press. From this, cut 2 (16¾") strips. Join borders to quilt sides with wider border at outside edge.
3. Join remaining border strips in same manner; press. From this strip set, cut 2 (13¼") borders. Join a ball block to each end of these borders. Sew borders to top and bottom edges of quilt.

Quilting and Finishing

1. Layer backing, batting, and quilt top; baste. Quilt as desired. Quilt shown has outline-quilting around dogs and balls and a cable pattern quilted in borders.
2. Fold each binding strip in half lengthwise, wrong sides facing, and press. Sew 1 pair of strips to quilt sides; trim even with top and bottom edges of quilt. Sew second pair of binding strips to top and bottom edges. Tuck ends under ¼" at corners and secure binding on back of quilt.

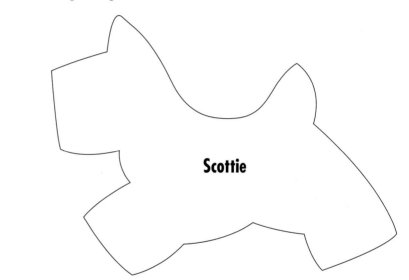

Scottie

Note: Patterns are finished-size and do not include seam allowances.

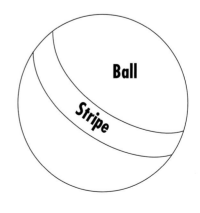

Ball

Stripe

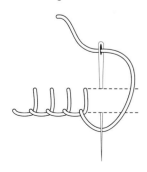

Blanket Stitch

French Knot

FANTASY FISH

Quilt by Roxanne Elliott of Trussville, Alabama;
machine-quilted by Lynn Witzenburg of Des Moines, Iowa

This quick-pieced quilt turns any room into a tropical paradise. Use one of today's popular mottled fabrics to provide a watery background for scrap-fabric fish. Choose jewel-tone fabrics like this example, or soft pastels for calmer seas.

Finished Size

Quilt: 72½" x 86"
Blocks: 9 (13½" x 18") Block 1
        30 (4½" x 6") Block 2

Materials

3⅜ yards water fabric
2⅛ yards outer border fabric
½ yard inner border fabric
14 (⅛-yard) pieces or scraps for fish
1 yard binding fabric
5½ yards backing fabric

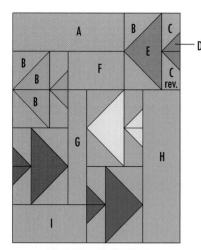

Block 1—Make 9.

Cutting

Instructions are for rotary cutting and quick piecing. Cut all strips cross-grain except as noted. For traditional cutting and piecing, use patterns on pages 17–19. Cut pieces in order listed to get best use of yardage.

From water fabric
- 27 (3½"-wide) strips. From these, cut:
    9 (3½" x 12½") H pieces.
    9 (3½" x 9½") A pieces.
    150 (3½") B squares.
    9 (3½" x 6½") I pieces.
    9 (3½" x 5") F pieces.
    150 (2" x 3½") C pieces.
- 1 (14"-wide) strip. From this, cut:
    1 (12½" x 14") Y piece.
    4 (6½" x 14") X pieces.
- 3 (2"-wide) strips. From these, cut:
    9 (2" x 9½") G pieces.
    2 (2" x 6½") Z pieces.

From outer border fabric
- 4 (9" x 75") lengthwise strips. Add remaining fabric to scraps for fish, if desired. Leftover fabric is enough for 13 Es and 26 matching Ds.

From inner border fabric
- 8 (2"-wide) strips.

*From scrap fabrics**
- 66 (3½" x 6½") E pieces.
- 18 (3½") B squares.
- 150 (2") D squares.

Note: Cut scrap fabrics in sets; 2 Bs and 2 Ds make 1 fish, or 1 E and 2 Ds make 1 fish.

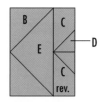

Block 2—Make 30.

Block Assembly

Refer to Block 1 Assembly Diagram throughout.

1. For each block, select 4 E/D sets of scrap fabrics and 1 B/D set. From water fabric, select 10 Bs, 10 Cs, and 1 each of A, F, G, H, and I.
2. On wrong side of a B water square, draw a diagonal line from corner to corner. Match a marked water square with each scrap B square, right sides facing. Stitch on drawn line (Diagram A). Trim excess fabric from corner, leaving a ¼" seam allowance from seam line. Press open.
3. See tips on Diagonal-Corners Quick-Piecing Method, page 11. Use this technique to sew B corners to each E piece (Diagram B) and D corners to each C (Diagram C). Be sure to sew 5 C/D units with seam angling right and 5 units with seam angling left as shown.
4. For Section 1, join a B/B square with a C/D unit and piece F. Sew

piece A to top of row. Press seam allowances toward A. Then sew B/E unit to end of row. Join 2 C/D units end-to-end to make fish tail as shown (Diagram D); join tail to B/E unit.
5. For Section 2, join remaining B square with its C/D unit. Join 2 C/D units; then join tail to 1 B/E fish. Sew B unit to top of B/E fish. Then sew piece G to right side as shown. Complete section with piece I at bottom.
6. For Section 3, assemble C/D tails and join to 2 B/E fish. Join fish as shown. Complete section with piece H at right side.
7. Join sections 2 and 3; then sew Section 1 at top to complete block. Press.
8. Make 9 of Block 1, varying scrap fabrics as desired.
9. Use remaining B, E, C, and D pieces to make 30 of Block 2 (Diagram D). *continued*

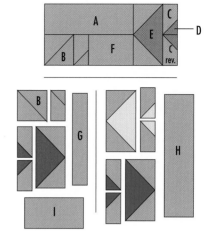

Block 1 Assembly Diagram

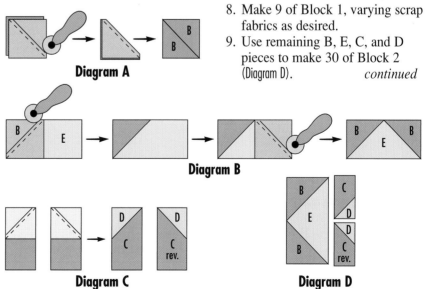

Diagram A

Diagram B

Diagram C

Diagram D

Quilt Assembly

1. Lay out large blocks in 3 vertical rows of 3 blocks each (Quilt Assembly Diagram). If desired, turn blocks upside down here and there to vary fish placement. Add X and Y pieces to rows as shown.
2. When satisfied with placement, join blocks and setting pieces in each row. Then join rows.

Borders

1. Measure width of quilt through middle of quilt top. Trim 2 inner border strips to this measurement. Stitch border strips to top and bottom edges of quilt.
2. Sew 2 remaining inner border strips end-to-end for each side border. Measure length of quilt through the middle and trim side borders to this length. Sew border strips to quilt sides, easing to fit as needed.
3. Select 15 of Block 2 for each side border. Join blocks side-by-side, inserting a Z piece somewhere in each row as shown (Quilt Assembly Diagram). Sew borders to quilt sides. (To allow for piecing variations, Zs can be omitted or more can be added to make border fit quilt).
4. Measure length of quilt as before and trim 2 outer border strips to match quilt length. Sew borders to quilt sides.
5. Measure quilt width through middle; trim remaining outer border strips to match quilt width. Sew borders to top and bottom edges.

Make a splash with a fish of a different color. Here are two suggestions for alternate views of Fantasy Fish.

Quilt Assembly Diagram

Pastel Alternate Color Scheme

Primary Alternate Color Scheme

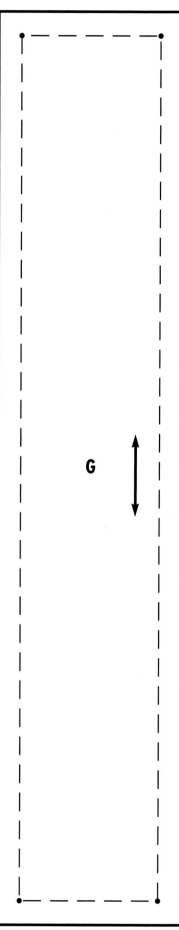

G

Quilting and Finishing

1. Mark quilt top with desired quilting design. Quilt shown is machine-quilted with repeated wavy lines quilted across the "ocean" and inner border. A commercial stencil was used to mark cable in outer border.

2. Layer backing, batting, and quilt top. Baste. Quilt as desired.
3. Make 9¼ yards of continuous straight-grain or bias binding. Bind quilt edges.

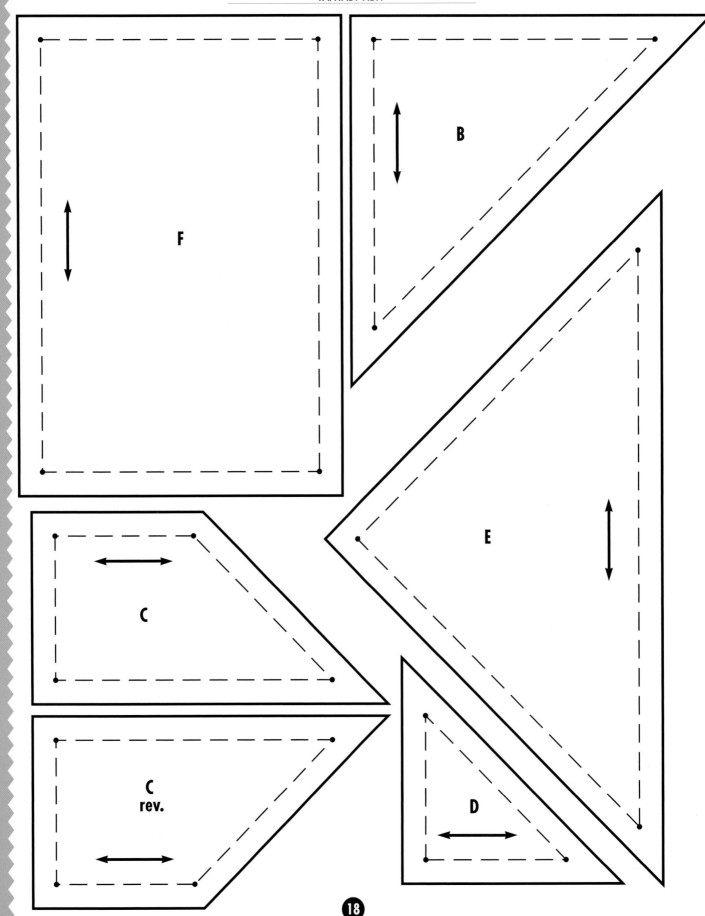

For Pattern H, draw a
rectangle 3½" x 12½".

H

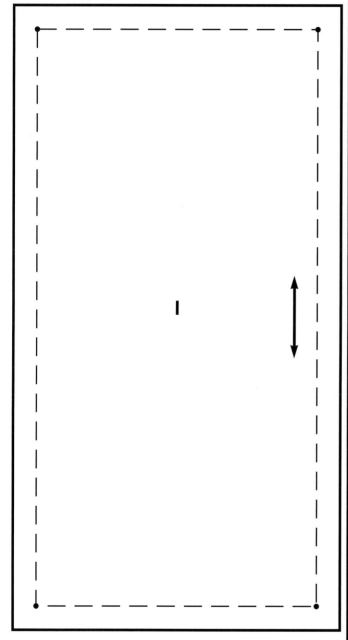

I

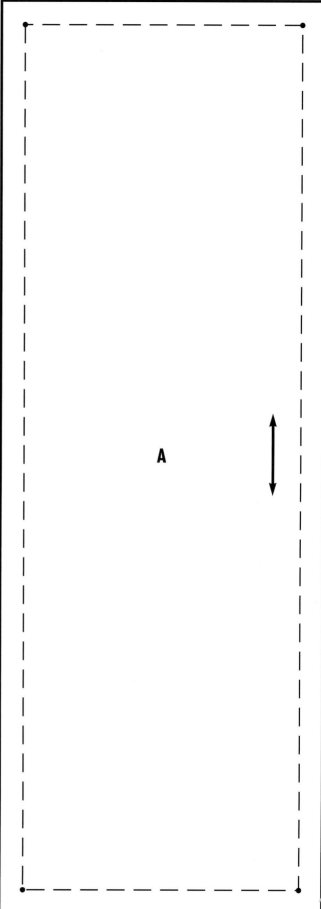

A

MARKET MEMORIES

Quilt by Joyce Stewart of Rexburg, Idaho

Joyce Stewart's memories of the 1992 Quilt Market in Houston, Texas, will stay forever fresh in this pretty quilt. Blue-and-gray Album blocks—which feature signatures of Market friends—alternate with scrapped-up Sheepfold blocks to create the linked chain design.

Finished Size

Quilt: 64" x 64"
Blocks: 81 (5" x 5")

Materials

400 (1¾") scrap squares
2 yards light blue print
3½ yards navy print
⅝ yard gray print
4 yards backing fabric

Cutting

Instructions are for rotary cutting. For traditional cutting and piecing, use patterns on pages 22 and 23.
From light blue print
• 4 (5" x 68") lengthwise strips for outer border.
• 6 (1½" x 36") lengthwise strips for middle border.

From navy fabric
• 4 (2" x 52") lengthwise strips for inner border.
• 6 (1" x 36") lengthwise strips for middle border.
• 2 (26") squares for bias appliqué and binding.
• 82 (3⅜") squares. Cut each square in half diagonally to get 164 A triangles.
• 180 (1¾" x 3") D pieces.
• 4 (3") E squares.
• 16 (3" x 5½") F pieces.
• 32 (2") G squares for appliqué.
• 40 (1¾") C squares.
From gray print
• 41 (4") B squares.

20

**Album Block—
Make 41.**

**Sheepfold Block—
Make 40.**

Album Blocks

1. Sew 2 A triangles to opposite sides of a B square (Diagram A). Press seam allowances toward triangles.
2. Sew 2 triangles to remaining sides of square to complete block (Diagram B). Press.
3. Make 41 Album blocks.

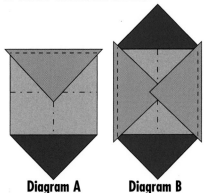

Diagram A   **Diagram B**

Sheepfold Blocks

1. For 1 block, select 8 scrap squares and 4 Ds.
2. For center four-patch, join 2 pairs of scrap squares (Diagram C); then join pairs to form a square.
3. Sew D pieces to opposite sides of four-patch. Press seam allowances toward Ds.
4. Sew squares to both ends of remaining Ds as shown. Press seam allowances toward Ds.

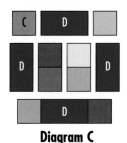

Diagram C

5. Join rows to complete block.
6. Make 40 Sheepfold blocks and 20 half-blocks (Diagram D).

Diagram D

Quilt Assembly

1. For Row 1, join 2 Es, 4 Fs, and 5 half-blocks (Row Assembly Diagram). Make 2 of Row 1.
2. For Row 2, join 5 Album blocks, 4 Sheepfold blocks, and 2 half-blocks. Make 5 of Row 2.
3. For Row 3, join 4 Album blocks, 5 Sheepfold blocks, and 2 Fs as shown. Make 4 of Row 3.
4. Referring to photo, join rows 1-2-3-2-3. Assemble second set of rows 1-2-3-2-3. To join, sew Row 3 of each set to opposite sides of remaining Row 2.

Borders

1. For inner border, sew navy strips to quilt edges and miter corners.
2. Join 2 (1"-wide) navy strips and 2 (1½"-wide) blue strips to make a strip set (Diagram E). Make 3 strip sets. From these, cut 72 (1½"-wide) segments for middle border.
3. Join 18 segments end-to-end to make each of 4 borders.
4. With right sides facing, match navy end of 1 border to top left corner of quilt. Sew border to top edge of quilt, stopping about 2" from right-hand corner.
5. Match light blue end of next border strip to top left corner and sew border to left edge of quilt.
6. Starting with light blue ends, sew border strips to bottom and right edges of quilt. When last border is added, complete seam for top border.
7. For outer border, sew light blue strips to quilt edges; miter corners.

continued

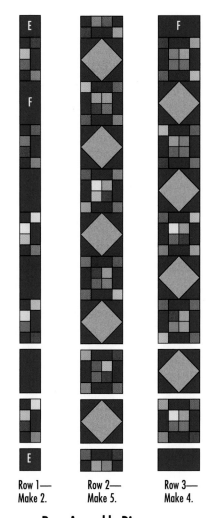

**Row 1—
Make 2.**   **Row 2—
Make 5.**   **Row 3—
Make 4.**

Row Assembly Diagram

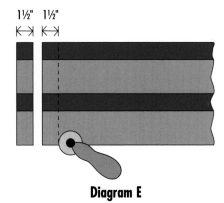

1½"   1½"

Diagram E

Appliqué

1. Turn under edges of each navy G square.
2. Starting at middle border corner, pin 8 squares on top light blue border, spacing them about 1¼" above middle border and 5¼" apart (point to point). Bottom point of each square should be in line with 1 small navy strip of middle border.
3. Use 1 (26") square of navy fabric to make bias for appliqué. Cut square in half diagonally to get 2 triangles. Measuring from cut edges, rotary-cut 1"-wide bias strips. From these strips, cut 64 (9"-long) pieces.
4. Because this bias is so narrow, it may be difficult to sew and press with bias bars. It's easier to fold each piece in half lengthwise, wrong sides facing, and press. Fold pressed strip lengthwise again so that fold overlaps raw edge slightly and press.
5. Referring to photo and Bias Placement Guide on this page, pin pressed strips in arcs between squares. At center of each arc, strips will be approximately 2½" apart. Tuck strip ends under squares.
6. Pin squares and bias strips in place on remaining borders. Use Bias Placement Guide to position strips for corners.
7. When satisfied with placement of all squares and bias strips, appliqué strips onto border fabric. Then stitch squares in place over strip ends.

Quilting and Finishing

1. Mark quilting design on quilt top as desired. Quilt shown is outline-quilted.
2. Layer backing, batting, and quilt top; baste. Quilt as desired.
3. Use remaining navy fabric to make 7½ yards of continuous bias or straight-grain binding. Bind quilt edges.

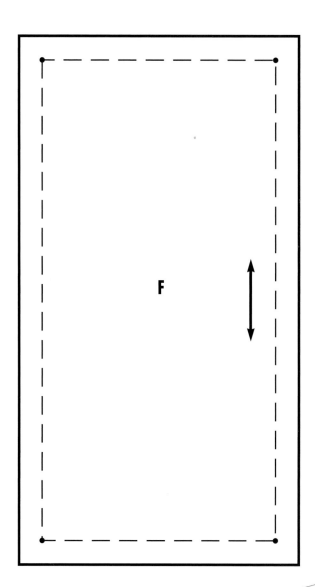

F

Bias Placement Guide

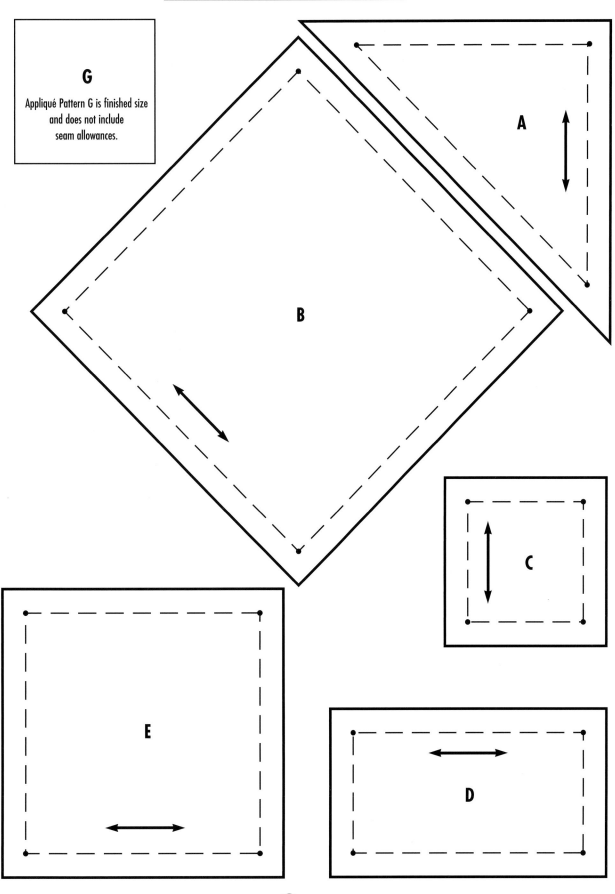

G

Appliqué Pattern G is finished size
and does not include
seam allowances.

A

B

C

E

D

DOUBLE T

Quilt by Diane J. Burdin of Batavia, Illinois

T Blocks were a popular symbol of the Temperance Movement, an effort by 19th-century women to abolish alcohol. Diane Burdin was attracted to the pattern after seeing an antique quilt displayed at a local book store. In keeping with vintage quilts, Diane varied the placement of lights and darks in her patchwork, making "maverick" blocks that keep the pattern interesting.

Finished Size
Quilt: 66" x 81¾"
Blocks: 20 (12¾" x 12¾")

Materials
15 fat eighths (9" x 22") assorted
   solid fabrics
20 fat eighths assorted print fabrics
⅜ yard orange for sashing squares
1¾ yards brown print for sashing
¾ yard binding fabric
5 yards backing fabric

Cutting
Cut all strips cross-grain. Several blocks in this quilt have 1 odd piece or 1 odd T in them. Instructions are given for matching blocks, but have fun and mix them if you like.
From assorted solids
• 80 (2" x 5") A rectangles in sets
  of 4.*
• 160 (2½") B squares in sets of 8.*
Note: Each block uses 4 A pieces and 8 Bs of matching fabric.
From each assorted print
• 8 (2" x 5") A rectangles.
• 1 (5") square (C).
• 1 (7⅝") square. Cut squares in
  quarters diagonally to get 4 D
  triangles.
• 2 (4⅛") squares. Cut squares in
  half diagonally to get 4 E triangles.
From orange
• 3 (3½"-wide) strips. From these,
  cut 30 (3½") squares for sashing.
From brown print
• 17 (3½"-wide) strips. From these,
  cut 49 (3½" x 13¼") sashings.

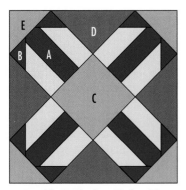

Double T Block—Make 20.

Block Assembly

1. For each block, choose 8 print A pieces and 4 solid As. Join 2 print pieces to both sides of 1 solid A to make a square (T Unit Diagram). Make 4 A units.
2. See page 11 for instructions on diagonal-corner technique. Using this method, sew solid Bs to top corners of each A unit as shown. Triangles will overlap center strip slightly. Make 4 T units.
3. Lay out 4 T units, 1 C, 4 Ds, and 4 Es (Block Assembly Diagram). Join units in diagonal rows as shown. Then join rows to complete block.
4. Make 20 T blocks.

continued

T Unit Diagram

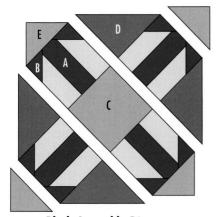

Block Assembly Diagram

Quilt Assembly

1. Lay out blocks in 5 horizontal rows, with 4 blocks and 5 sashing strips in each row (Block Row Diagram). Make 5 block rows.
2. Join 5 sashing squares and 4 sashing strips into a row (Sashing Row Diagram). Make 6 sashing rows.
3. Referring to photo, alternate sashing rows and block rows. Join rows to complete quilt top.

Quilting and Finishing

1. Mark quilting designs on quilt top as desired. On quilt shown, patchwork is quilted in-the-ditch. Pattern for C square is on this page. Create your own quilting design for sashing strips or look for an available stencil that fits that area.
2. Layer backing, batting, and quilt top; baste. Quilt as desired.
3. Make 8½ yards of continuous bias or straight-grain binding. Bind quilt edges.

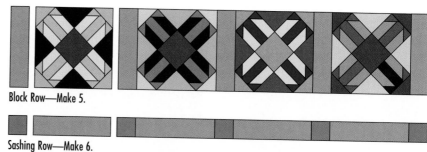

Block Row—Make 5.

Sashing Row—Make 6.

Row Assembly Diagram

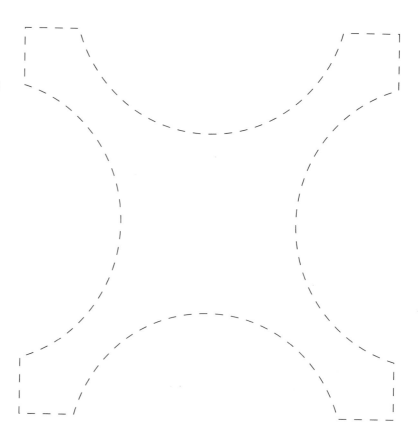

Center Quilting Pattern

WORKING WITH BIAS EDGES

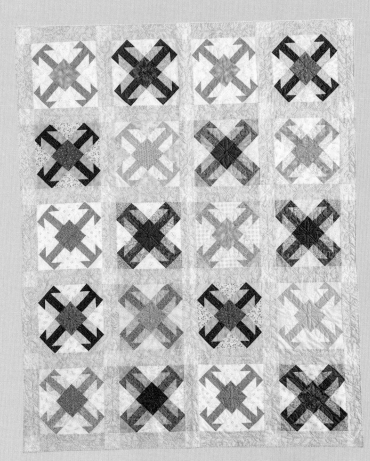

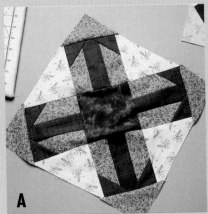

A

B

C

D

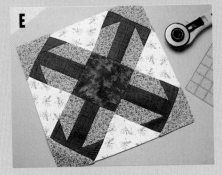

E

Rhonda Richards made a version of Double T in a pastel color scheme. In the process, she came up with a helpful tip.

Some of Rhonda's blocks were a little wobbly in the center *(photo A)*.

Rather than lying flat, the center square raised off the table a bit. Rhonda realized she wasn't handling the D pieces carefully. Those triangles are bias on two sides, and they can stretch during sewing and pressing. When this happens, the block won't lie flat.

To fix the problem, Rhonda pinned each corner of the block to a ruled ironing surface *(photo B)*. This ensures that you don't stretch your block beyond the size it's supposed to be. Then she sprayed enough starch on the block to make it damp *(photo C)*. If you don't like starch, mist your block with water. With your iron set on "steam," gently press the block flat and to size *(photo D)*. Begin in the center, and slowly move outward to press it flat. The steam reshapes the block and redistributes the "roomy" areas so the block will lie flat *(photo E)*.

Use this trick with care—if you get carried away, you'll stretch the block out of shape and make it too big. But with a little careful pressing, you can repair minor mistakes.

IRISH CHAIN

Quilt by Winnie Fleming of Houston, Texas;
hand-quilted by Evelyn Anthony of South Houston, Texas

Classic design meets contemporary fabrics in this sparkling version of a perennial favorite. Ideal for quick-piecing techniques, this gem is a showcase for best-loved fabrics and offers great opportunities to show off pretty quilting designs.

Finished Size

Quilt: 82" x 92"
Blocks: 35 (10" x 10")

Materials

5 yards white or muslin
100 (2½" x 21") strips jewel-tone print fabrics
2¾ yards 90"-wide backing fabric

Cutting

Cut all strips cross-grain unless specified otherwise.
From white fabric
• 32" square for binding.
• 4 (5½" x 85") lengthwise strips for outer borders.
• 17 (6½" x 10½") pieces for Block B, from waste left from border cut.
• 8 (2½"-wide) strips for inner borders.
• 4 (4½" x 21") strips for Strip Set 4.
• 10 (2½" x 21") strips for strip sets.

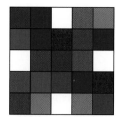

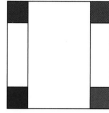

Block A—Make 18.

Block B—Make 17.

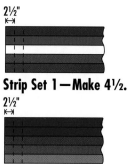

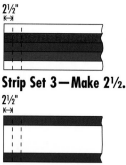

Strip Set 1—Make 4½.

Strip Set 3—Make 2½.

Strip Set 2—Make 4½.

Strip Set 4—Make 4.

Block Assembly

1. For Strip Set 1, join 4 print strips and 1 white strip (Strip Set 1 Diagram). Press all seam allowances toward center white strip. Make 4 of Strip Set 1, varying fabrics. Cut 4 scrap strips and 1 white strip in half to make a half-set.

2. Cut 8 (2½"-wide) segments from each set (4 from half-set) to get a total of 36 Strip Set 1 segments. (To keep cut pieces safe, put each batch in a zip-top plastic bag; then you can label the bag to easily identify its contents later.)

3. For Strip Set 2, select 5 scrap strips. Join strips as shown (Strip Set 2 Diagram). Press all seam allowances away from center strip. Make 4 of Strip Set 2, varying scrap fabrics. Cut 5 scrap strips in half to make a half-set.

4. Cut 8 (2½"-wide) segments from each set (4 from half-set) to get 36 Strip Set 2 segments.

5. For Strip Set 3, join 3 scrap strips and 2 white strips as shown (Strip Set 3 Diagram). Press all seam allowances toward center strip. Make 2½ of Strip Set 3, varying fabrics. Cut 2½"-wide segments to get 18 Strip Set 3 segments.

6. For Block A, select 1 Strip Set 3 segment and 2 each of segments 1 and 2. Arrange strips as shown (Block A Assembly Diagram). Join strips to complete block. Make 18 of Block A, varying scrap fabrics.

7. For Strip Set 4, select 2 scrap strips and 1 (4½"-wide) white strip. Join strips as shown (Strip Set 4 Diagram). Press seam allowances away from white. Make 4 of Strip Set 4, varying scrap fabrics.

8. Cut 2½"-wide segments to get 16 Strip Set 4 segments. Use leftover fabrics to piece 2 more segments.

9. For Block B, select 2 Strip Set 4 segments and 1 (6½" x 10½") white piece. Join strips as shown. Make 17 of Block B.

Quilt Assembly

1. Lay out 7 horizontal rows of 5 blocks each, alternating A blocks and B blocks (Row Assembly Diagram). Lay out 4 of Row 1, starting with an A block. Then lay out 3 of Row 2, starting with a B block.

2. When satisfied with placement, join blocks in each row.

3. Join rows, alternating rows as shown in photo.

Borders

1. Sew 2 white strips end-to-end for each inner border. Measure length of quilt; then trim 2 border strips to match length. Sew these to quilt sides. Measure quilt width and trim remaining border strips to match. Join borders to top and

bottom edges of quilt. Press seam allowances toward borders.

2. Join remaining scrap strips in pairs. You should have enough strips left to sew 17 pairs. Press.

3. From these strip sets, cut 136 (2½"-wide) pair segments.

4. Referring to photo, join 37 pairs in a vertical row for each side border. Sew pieced borders to quilt sides, easing to fit.

5. Join 31 pairs in a row for top border. Sew pieced border to top edge of quilt, easing to fit. Repeat for bottom border.

6. Measure length of quilt and trim 2 outer border strips to fit. Sew these to quilt sides. Then measure quilt width and trim remaining borders to fit. Sew borders to top and bottom edges of quilt.

Quilting and Finishing

1. Mark quilting designs on quilt top as desired. Make your own design or look for available stencils of pretty designs that will fit borders and Block B center.

2. Layer backing, batting, and quilt top. Baste. Quilt as desired.

3. Make 10 yards of continuous bias or straight-grain binding. Bind quilt edges.

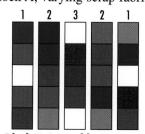

Block A Assembly Diagram

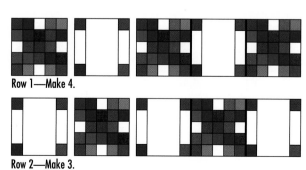

Row 1—Make 4.

Row 2—Make 3.

Row Assembly Diagram

TWINKLING STARS

Quilt by Carole Braig of Des Peres, Missouri

When Ellen Sweeney came to visit her friend Carole Braig, they went quilt-shop hopping, buying red and white fabrics to make quilts. During Ellen's visit, they took turns cutting and sewing cheerful Sawtooth Star blocks.

"Ellen called after she got home to say that it wasn't much fun sewing alone—could I come play?" Carole remembers. Both finished their quilts alone, but "she was right," says Carole. "It wasn't as much fun as making stars with a friend."

Finished Size
Quilt: 93½" x 93½"
Blocks: 100 (8" x 8")

Materials
34 fat quarters (18" x 22") red prints
10 (½-yard) pieces light prints
⅜ yard red print for inner border
½ yard cream print for middle border
9¼ yards black-on-red print for outer border, binding, and backing

Cutting
Cut strips cross-grain except as noted.
From red prints
- 93 (7" x 18") pieces. From *each* of these, cut 1 (4½") A square and 8 (2½") C squares. Keep each set intact for 1 Sawtooth Star block or mix pieces for scrappier blocks.
- 7 (7" x 18") pieces. From *each* of these, cut 8 (2½") C squares, 1 (2½") E square, and 8 (1½") G squares. Designate 1 set for each Double Star block, or mix fabrics as desired.

From light prints
- 69 (2½"-wide) strips. From these, cut 400 (2½" x 4½") B pieces, 400 (2½") D squares, and 28 (1½" x 2½") F pieces.
- 1 (1½"-wide) strip. From this, cut 28 (1½") H squares.

From red border print
- 8 (1¼"-wide) strips for inner border.

From cream print
- 8 (1¾"-wide) strips for middle border.

From black-on-red print
- 33" square for binding.
- 2 (5" x 88") and 2 (5" x 99") lengthwise strips for outer border.
- 1 (18" x 99") and 2 (40" x 99") lengthwise strips for backing.

Block Assembly

Refer to Block Assembly Diagram throughout.

1. For each Sawtooth Star block, select 1 A square, 4 Bs, 8 C squares, and 4 D squares. Fabrics can match or vary, as desired.
2. Use diagonal-corners technique (page 11) to join 2 Cs to each B (Diagram A). Make 4 B/C units for each block.
3. Join units in 3 horizontal rows as shown. Join rows to complete block. Make 93 blocks.
4. For each Double Star block, select 1 E, 4 Fs, 8 Gs, 4 Hs, 4 Bs, 8 Cs, and 4 Ds.
5. Use diagonal-corners method to make 4 B/C units and 4 F/G units. Join E, F/G, and H units to make block center in same manner as Sawtooth Star. Then add B/C units and Ds to complete block. Make 7 blocks (Double Star Block Diagram).

Quilt Assembly

Refer to Quilt Assembly Diagram throughout.

1. Lay out blocks in 10 rows, with 10 blocks in each row. Place Double Star blocks as desired.
2. Join blocks in each row. Then join rows. *continued*

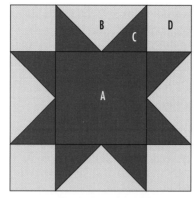

Sawtooth Star Block—Make 93.

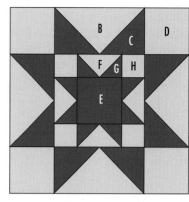

Double Star Block—Make 7.

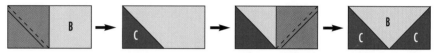

Diagram A

Quilt Assembly Diagram

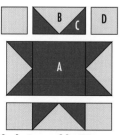

Block Assembly Diagram

Borders

1. Join 2 red print strips end-to-end to assemble each border.
2. Measuring through middle of quilt, measure quilt from top to bottom. Trim 2 borders to match length. Sew strips to quilt sides.
3. Measure width of quilt. Trim 2 borders to fit and sew to top and bottom edges.
4. Repeat steps 1, 2, and 3 to assemble and sew cream borders to quilt top.
5. Add black-on-red print border in same manner.

Quilting and Finishing

1. Mark quilting designs on quilt top as desired. Quilt shown is outline-quilted by machine, with an X stitched across each A and D square. A simple cable is hand-quilted in borders.
2. Assemble backing. Layer backing, batting, and quilt top; baste. Quilt as desired.
3. Make 10⅝ yards of continuous bias or straight-grain binding. Bind quilt edges.

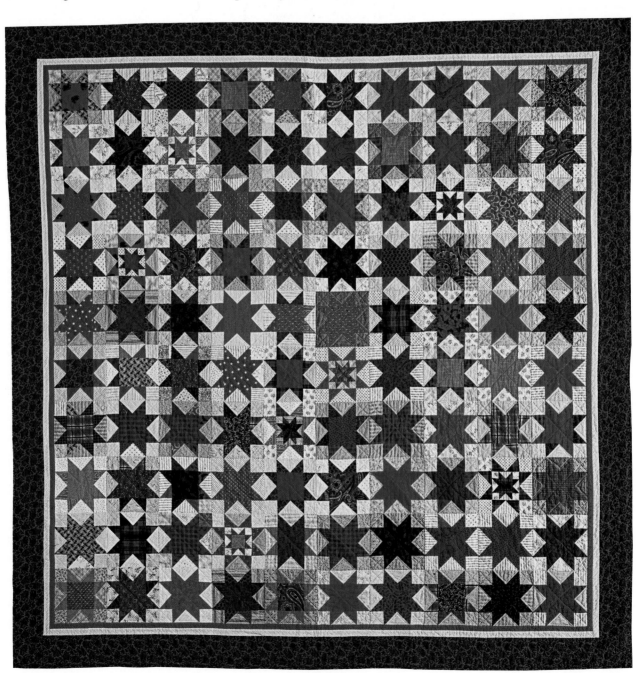

PATRIOTIC RAIL FENCE

Quilt by Rhonda Richards of Birmingham, Alabama;
quilted by Sharon Wilson of Montgomery, Alabama

R honda Richards was one of many
Southerners who had Olympic
fever during the 1996 summer games
in Atlanta. "With the games here in
our own backyard, it seemed every-
one caught the Olympic spirit," says
Rhonda. "I wanted to make a quilt to
commemorate that summer. I had a
lot of Americana prints, so Rail
Fence was a natural—it was easy to
strip-piece them together." Rail Fence
is a quick and easy quilt to use lots of
scraps in any three-color scheme.

Finished Size

Quilt: 102" x 102"
Blocks: 400 (4½" x 4½")

Materials

100 (2" x 22") red print strips
100 (2" x 22") cream print strips
100 (2" x 22") blue print strips
1¼ yards navy solid fabric for inner
    border and binding
3 yards stripe border fabric
3 yards 108"-wide backing fabric

Cutting

From navy solid
• 9 (2" x 42") strips for inner border.
• 10 (2¼" x 42") strips for straight-
  grain binding.
From border stripe
• 4 (5"-wide) lengthwise strips.
continued

Block Assembly

1. Join 1 strip each of red, cream, and blue into a strip set (Diagram A). Make 100 strip sets. Press seam allowances away from cream strip.

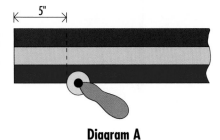

Diagram A

2. Cut 4 (5"-wide) segments from each segment to get 400 Rail Fence blocks.

Quilt Assembly

1. Lay out blocks in 20 horizontal rows, with 20 blocks in each row (Row Assembly Diagram). For Row 1 and all odd-numbered rows, turn first block vertically with red strip on left. Make 10 odd rows. For Row 2 and all even-numbered rows, turn first block horizontally with red strip at top. Make 10 even rows. In all rows, press seam allowances toward vertical blocks.

2. Join rows, alternating odd and even, to complete quilt center (Quilt Assembly Diagram).

Borders

1. Cut 1 navy border strip into 4 equal pieces. Join 1 quarter piece and 2 full-width strips end-to-end to make a border strip for each quilt side.

2. Measuring through middle of quilt, measure quilt from top to bottom. Trim 2 border strips to matching length. Sew strips to quilt sides. Press seam allowances toward borders.

3. Measure width of quilt. Trim 2 remaining borders to fit and sew to top and bottom edges.

4. Measure, trim, and add stripe borders to quilt in same manner.

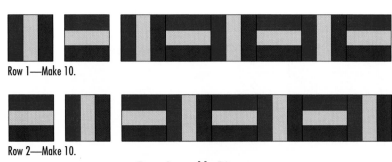

Row 1—Make 10.

Row 2—Make 10.

Row Assembly Diagram

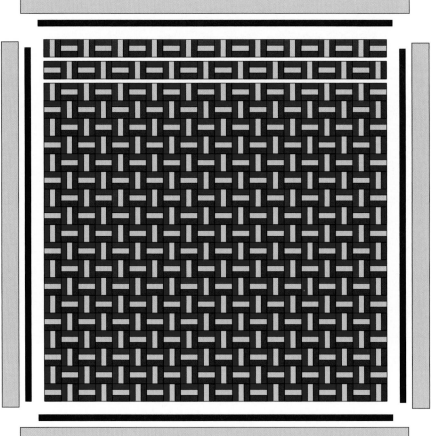

Quilt Assembly Diagram

Quilting and Finishing

1. Mark quilting designs on quilt top as desired. Quilt shown is machine-quilted in an allover loop design and stipple quilting in borders.

2. Layer backing, batting, and quilt top; baste. Quilt as desired.

3. Join binding strips end-to-end to make 11½ yards of continuous straight-grain binding. Bind quilt edges.

Variable Sizes

The quilt shown fits a king-size bed. However, this pattern is easily adapted to fit any bed. Use the chart below as a starting point.

Size	Wall/Crib	Twin	Double	Queen
Finished Size	34½" x 43½"	66" x 93"	79½" x 93"	84" x 102"
Number of Blocks	35	216	270	320
Blocks Set	5 x 7	12 x 18	15 x 18	16 x 20

STARS & CROSSES

Quilt by Linda Esslinger Winter of Holdrege, Nebraska

This quilt reminds Linda Winter of her great aunt, Alma Esslinger. Linda used feedsacks that belonged to Alma to make a quilt in her aunt's memory. "I quilted a rose trellis in the borders," says Linda, "because my aunt had beautiful rose gardens."

The stars you see in this quilt appear only when the pieced cross blocks are joined. If you don't have a collection of authentic feedsacks, reproduction prints work just as well.

Finished Size
Quilt: 101" x 101"
Blocks: 36 (14" x 14")

Materials
20 fat eighths (9" x 22") medium and dark prints
14 fat eighths light prints
6¼ yards white or muslin
2 yards pink print for outer border and binding
½ yard blue print for inner border
3 yards 108"-wide backing fabric

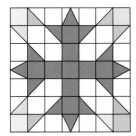

Cross Block—Make 20.

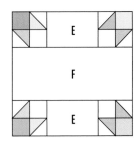

Setting Block—Make 16.

Corner Unit Diagram

Cutting

Cut all strips cross-grain except as noted. Make templates for patterns B and C on page 38. Cut pieces in order listed to get most efficient use of yardage.

From each medium/dark fabric
• 9 (2½") A squares.
• 4 of Pattern B.
• 4 (2⅞") squares. Cut squares in half diagonally to get 8 D triangles. You will have 20 A/B/D sets, 1 for each block. Add remaining fabric to lights for additional patches.

From light fabrics and leftover mediums
• 28 (2⅞" x 22") strips. From these, cut 196 (2⅞") squares. Cut squares in half diagonally to get 392 D triangles.
• 25 (2½" x 22") strips. From these, cut 196 (2½") A squares.

From white
• 10 (6½"-wide) strips. From these, cut 16 (6½" x 14½") F pieces and 56 (4½" x 6½") E pieces.
• 28 (2½"-wide) strips. From these, cut 436 (2½") A squares.
• 80 of Pattern C.
• 80 of Pattern C reversed.
• 19 (2⅞"-wide) strips. Cut strips into 276 (2⅞") squares. Cut squares in half diagonally to get 552 D triangles.

From blue print
• 10 (1½"-wide) strips.

From pink print
• 10 (4"-wide) strips.
• 11 (2½"-wide) strips for binding.

Cross Block Assembly

Refer to Cross Block Assembly Diagram throughout.
1. Select 1 block set of A/B/D pieces. Join 5 print A squares and 4 white A squares to make a nine-patch unit (Nine-Patch Diagram).

Nine-Patch Diagram

2. Join 1 C and 1 C reversed to B (Point Unit Diagram). Press seam allowances toward Cs.
3. For each Side Unit, join print D triangles and white Ds to make 2 triangle-square units (Side Unit Diagram). Sew these to opposite sides

Point Unit Diagram   **Side Unit Diagram**

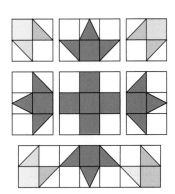

Cross Block Assembly Diagram

of print A square, positioning triangles as shown. Sew 2 white A squares to sides of Point Unit. Join rows to complete Side Unit. Make 4 units for each block.
4. For each Corner Unit, make 2 triangle-square units, using white Ds and light print Ds (Corner Unit Diagram). Join these to 1 light print A square and 1 white A as shown. Make 4 Corner Units.
5. Join 4 Side Units, nine-patch, and 4 Corner Units to make 1 block.
6. Make 20 blocks, using a set of print A/B/D pieces for each block.

Setting Block Assembly

Refer to Setting Block Assembly Diagram throughout.
1. Make 64 more Corner Units for Setting Blocks.
2. Select 4 units for each block. Sew 2 Corner Units to opposite ends of 2 E pieces. Press seam allowances toward E.
3. Sew corner rows to 1 F to complete block. Press seam allowances toward F.
4. Make 16 Setting Blocks.

continued

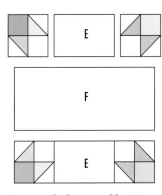

Setting Block Assembly Diagram

Border Unit Assembly

Make 52 Corner Units as before. Join 1 unit to each end of 1 E (Border Unit Assembly Diagram). Make 24 Border Units. Remaining 4 Corner Units will be border corners.

E

Border Unit Assembly Diagram

Quilt Assembly

Refer to Quilt Assembly Diagram throughout.

1. Lay out blocks in 6 horizontal rows of 6 blocks each, alternating Cross Blocks and Setting Blocks as shown. Rearrange blocks until you achieve a nice balance of color and value. Then join blocks in each row. Press seam allowances toward Setting Blocks.
2. Join rows to complete quilt center.
3. Join 2 rows of Border Units, with 6 units in each row. Sew 1 strip to each quilt side, matching seams. Make 2 more rows of Border Units, adding Corner Units to row ends. Add rows to top and bottom of quilt, matching seams.

Borders

1. Cut 2 blue border strips in half. Join 2 strips plus 1 half strip to make a border for each quilt side.
2. Measuring through middle of quilt, measure quilt from top to bottom. Trim 2 borders to match length. Sew strips to quilt sides.
3. Measure width of quilt. Trim remaining 2 borders to fit and sew to top and bottom edges.
4. Sew pink outer borders to quilt top in same manner.

Quilt Assembly Diagram

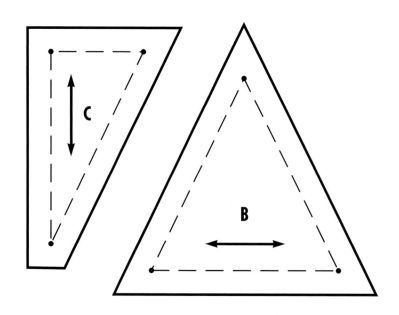

Quilting and Finishing

1. Mark quilting designs on quilt top as desired. Quilt shown is outline-quilted and background is filled with a diagonal grid pattern.

2. Layer backing, batting, and quilt top; baste. Quilt as desired.

3. Join pink strips into 1 continuous piece for straight-grain binding. Bind quilt edges.

QUEEN'S JEWELS

Quilt by Winnie Fleming of Houston, Texas;
machine-quilted by Barb Sawyer of Friendswood, Texas

This gem of a quilt is fast, easy, and *sew* much fun. Just cut and stitch strips of jewel-tone fabrics; then cut pre-pieced units that you can quickly assemble into blocks. If you prefer a homespun look, imagine this design in assorted plaids and earthy prints.

Finished Size

Quilt: 61½" x 77½"
Blocks: 12 (14½" x 14½")

Materials

2 yards black
2 yards white-on-white print
96 (2" x 18") scrap strips for blocks*
112 (2½") squares for borders*
4 yards backing fabric
* These pieces can be cut from 12 fat quarters, if desired.

Cutting

Instructions are for rotary cutting and strip piecing. For traditional cutting and piecing, use patterns on page 43. Cut all strips cross-grain except as noted.
From white fabric
• 6 (2½"-wide) strips for borders.
• 48 (2" x 18") strips for blocks.
From black fabric
• 4 (5" x 72") lengthwise strips for outer borders.
• 2 (2¾" x 72") lengthwise strips for inner side borders.
• 2 (3½" x 72") lengthwise strips for inner end borders.
• 4 (2½" x 72") lengthwise strips for straight-grain binding.

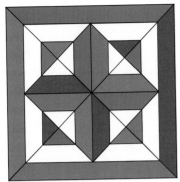

Night and Day Block—Make 12.

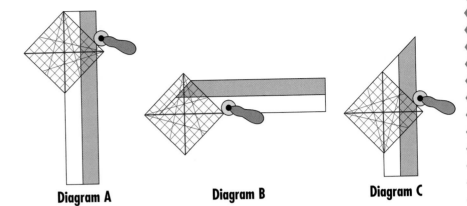

Diagram A   **Diagram B**   **Diagram C**

Block Assembly

The historic name of this block is Night and Day.

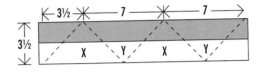

Diagram D

Diagram E

1. Join each 2" x 18" white strip to a matching strip of scrap fabric, making a strip set 3½" wide. Press seam allowances toward scrap fabric.

2. Use a square ruler that has a 45° line. Match line with white edge at one end of strip set (Diagram A). Trim corner as shown.

3. Turn cutting mat to position cut edge to your left (or right, if you're left-handed). With 45° line on edge of white fabric, slide ruler up to align its edge with top corner (Diagram B). Cut triangle.

4. Turn strip again as shown (Diagram C), aligning ruler with corner and white edge of strip set to cut next triangle. Continue cutting triangles in this manner; turn strip or mat as needed to align ruler.

Diagram F

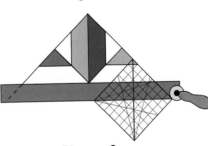

Diagram G

5. From each strip set, cut 2 X triangles with colored tips and 2 Y triangles with white tips (Diagram D) to get 96 of each. To make selection of triangles random, put Xs and Ys in separate bags or pillowcases. Reach in blind to select triangles as you make each block.

6. Each block has 4 sections. For each section, select 2 X triangles, 2 Ys, and 1 (2" x 18") scrap strip.

7. Join 2 Ys to make a square (Diagram E). Add Xs to sides of square to make a large triangle (Diagram F).

8. Matching centers, sew strip to bottom edge of triangle, letting strip extend at both ends. Press seam allowance toward bottom strip. Align edge of ruler with edge of triangle, matching 45° line with bottom (Diagram G). Trim strip ends at matching angle.

9. Join sections in pairs (Block Assembly Diagram); then join pairs to complete block. Make 12 blocks.

continued

Block Assembly Diagram

Quilt Assembly

1. Lay out blocks in 4 horizontal rows, with 3 blocks in each row. Arrange blocks to achieve a pleasing balance of color and contrast.
2. Join blocks in each row. Then join rows.

Flying Geese Border

Use diagonal-corner technique to make Flying Geese units (see page 11). This method is faster and easier for most people than cutting and sewing triangles.

1. From 2½"-wide white strips, cut 52 (2½" x 4½") pieces.
2. Use 2½" scrap squares to sew corners onto each rectangle (Diagram H). Make 52 Flying Geese units.

Diagram H

3. Referring to photo, join 15 Flying Geese units in a row for each side border. Join 11 units each for top and bottom borders. Sew 1 remaining scrap square to ends of each border.

Borders

1. Measuring through middle of quilt, measure quilt from top to bottom. Trim 2¾"-wide black strips to matching length. Sew strips to quilt sides.
2. Measure width of quilt. Trim 3½"-wide black borders to fit and sew to top and bottom edges.
3. Pin Flying Geese borders to sides, matching centers and ends. Sew borders to quilt sides, easing to fit as necessary. Repeat for top and bottom borders.
4. Cut 2 (5") squares from remaining white fabric. Cut squares in half diagonally to get 4 triangles. With right sides facing, center a triangle at each corner (Diagram I). Stitch through all layers. Press triangle to right side and check to see that it aligns with border correctly. (Triangles are oversized; trim as needed.) Cut excess fabric from seam allowances.
5. Repeat steps 1 and 2 to sew outer borders to quilt top.

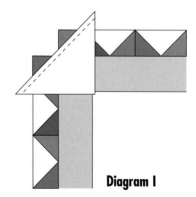

Diagram I

Quilting and Finishing

1. Mark quilting designs on quilt top as desired. Quilt shown is machine-quilted in an allover design, with hearts and cables quilted in borders.
2. Layer backing, batting, and quilt top; baste. Quilt as desired.
3. Join remaining black strips end-to-end to make 8 yards of continuous straight-grain binding. Bind quilt edges.

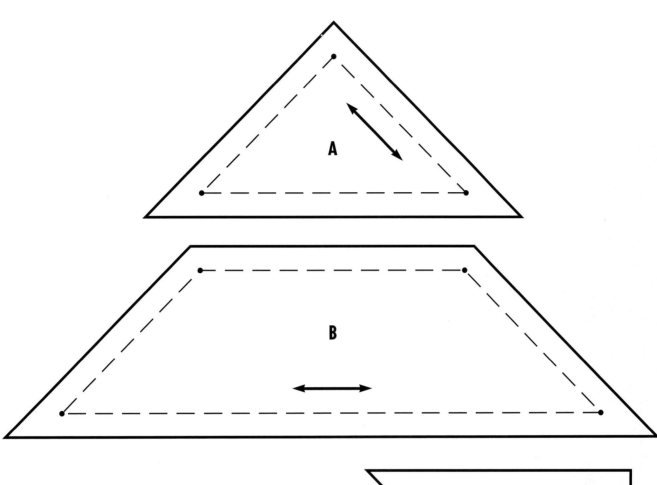

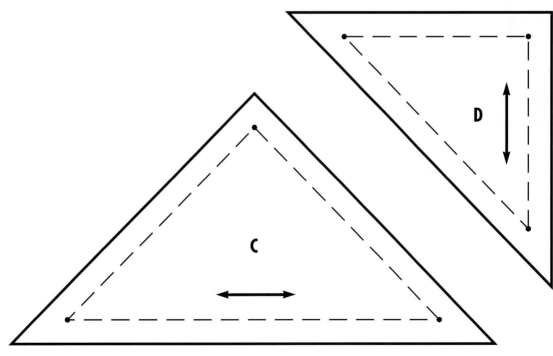

CABIN IN THE WOODS

Quilt by Bette Haddon of New Port Richey, Florida

Whether you see this bucolic setting as cabins in the country or a suburban subdivision, you can customize a patchwork neighborhood to suit your fancy. A consistent sky fabric unifies the scrappy blocks.

Finished Size

Quilt: 82" x 92"
Blocks: 27 (10" x 10") cabin blocks
  58 (5" x 10") tree blocks

Materials

2⅜ yards sky fabric
3 (6"-wide) green print strips
8 (5½"-wide) green print strips
25 (1½"-wide) green print strips
4 (1½"-wide) brown print strips
7 (13" x 16") gold print scraps
11 (1½" x 22") gold print strips
27 (6" x 12") red print scraps
32 (1½" x 22") red print strips
2¾ yards 90"-wide backing fabric
⅞ yard binding fabric

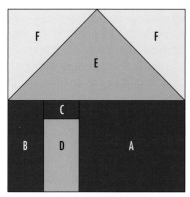

Block 1—Make 15.

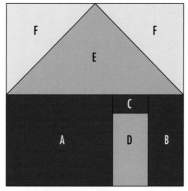

Block 2—Make 12.

Strip Set Diagram

Cutting

Instructions are for rotary cutting and quick piecing. Cut all strips cross-grain except as noted. Make templates of patterns J, K, M, and N on pages 47 and 48. Cut pieces in order listed to get best use of yardage.

From sky fabric
- 4 (5⅞"-wide) strips. From these, cut 27 (5⅞") squares. Cut each square in half diagonally to get 54 F triangles.
- 8 (2½"-wide) strips for Strip Set.
- 6 (4"-wide) strips. From these, cut 14 of Pattern J and 14 of Pattern J reversed.
- 2 (5½"-wide) strips. From these and remaining scraps, cut 4 (5½") L squares, 14 (2½" x 5½") I pieces, 4 of Pattern N, and 4 of Pattern N reversed.

From 6"-wide green print strips
- 14 of Pattern K.

From 5½"-wide green print strips
- 26 (5½" x 7½") G pieces.
- 14 (5½" x 6½") H pieces.
- 4 of Pattern M.

From each gold print scrap
- 1 (1½" x 16") strip for border.
- 1 (11¼") square. Cut each square in quarters diagonally to get a total of 27 E triangles (and 1 extra).
- 4 (2½" x 4½") D pieces (includes 1 extra).

From each red print scrap
- 1 (5½" x 6½") A piece.
- 1 (2½" x 5½") B piece.
- 1 (1½" x 2½") C piece.

House Block Assembly

1. Sew F triangles to both short legs of each E triangle (Block 1 Diagram). Press seam allowances toward Fs.
2. Join C piece to top edge of each D piece. Press seam allowances toward C.
3. For Block 1, sew A piece to right edge of C/D. Then sew B to left edge. Press seam allowances toward A and B.
4. Join E/F unit to top of each A/B/C/D unit to complete block. Make 15 of Block 1.
4. For Block 2, reverse position of A and B pieces (Block 2 Diagram). Complete block in same manner as for Block 1. Make 12 of Block 2.

Tree Block Assembly

Refer to block diagrams throughout.
1. Sew 2 (2½"-wide) sky fabric strips to both sides of each brown strip to get 4 strip sets (Strip Set Diagram). Press seam allowances toward brown.
2. From strip sets, cut 26 (3½"-wide) tree trunk segments for Block 3. Sew a G piece to top edge of each segment to complete block. Make 26 of Block 3.
3. For Block 4, sew an I sky piece to each H piece. Press seam allowance toward H. Then cut 28 (2½"-wide) trunk segments from strip set. Sew 14 segments to bottom of each H to make 14 of Block 4. (Use remaining segments for Block 5.)
4. For Block 5, sew J and J reversed pieces to both sides of each K piece. Press seam allowances toward Js. Sew a trunk segment to bottom of each J/K unit to make 14 of Block 5.
5. Sew N and N reversed pieces to both sides of each M piece. Press seam allowances toward Ns. Sew an L piece to top edge of tree. From remainder of strip set, cut 4 (1½"-wide) segments. Sew these to bottom edge of M/N units to complete 4 of Block 6.

continued

Block 3—Make 26.

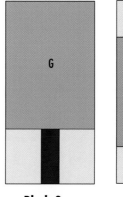

Block 4—Make 14.

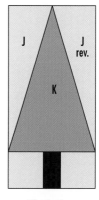

Block 5—Make 14.

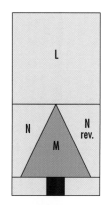

Block 6—Make 4.

Quilt Assembly

1. Lay out blocks in 8 horizontal rows (Quilt Assembly Diagram). When satisfied with placement, join blocks in each row. Press seam allowances toward tree blocks.
2. Join rows to complete quilt center.

Borders

1. Cut 1½"-wide gold strips into pieces of varying lengths.
2. Join gold strips end-to-end to make 2 pieced border strips 96" long and 2 pieced border strips 86" long. In same manner, make 4 red borders of each length and 6 green borders of each length.
3. For each side border, join 1 gold, 2 red, and 3 green 96"-long strips. Join 86"-long strips in same manner for top and bottom borders.
4. Sew borders to quilt edges, with gold strip against edge of quilt center, and miter corners. Press seam allowances toward borders.

Quilting and Finishing

Quilt 1" crosshatch pattern across entire quilt, or quilt as desired.

Make 10 yards of bias or straight-grain binding. Bind with bias binding made from dark green.

Quilt Assembly Diagram

N

½ M

Place on fold.

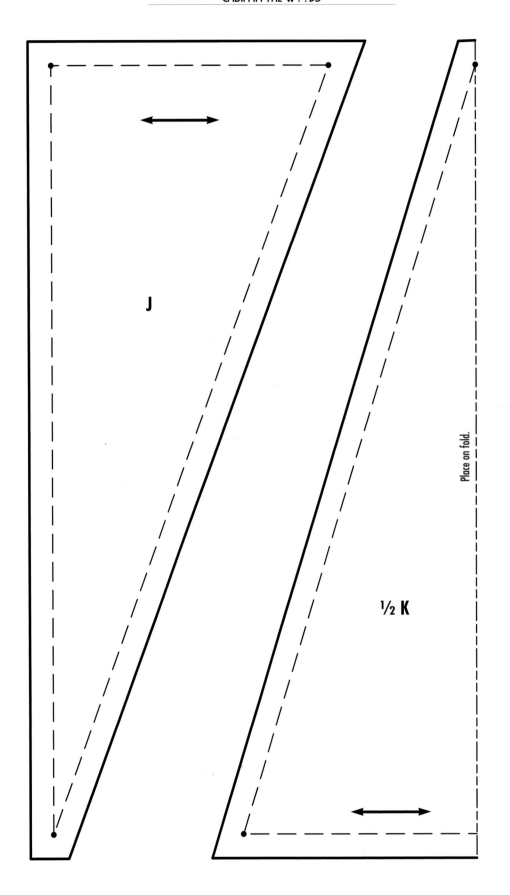

J

Place on fold.

½ K

SPARKS: JULY

This tipped star block is an example of the unexpected colorplay Rebecca Rohrkaste likes to invest in her quilts. She first made some of these blocks during a quilting weekend with friends and then put them aside for more than a year. When she pulled them out again, Rebecca eliminated some blocks, made new ones, and reworked others to get the effect she wanted. Working on the quilt during a July 4th weekend, Rebecca decided the blocks "look like fireworks or hot summer stars." She gave the quilt its name because of this illusion.

Finished Size

Quilt: 60" x 72"
Blocks: 30 (12" x 12")

Materials

30 (11" x 22") pieces purple, gold, and orange prints
30 (10" x 16") dark prints
4 yards backing fabric
¾ yard purple binding fabric

Cutting

Make templates of patterns B, C, D, and E on page 51.
From each 11" x 22" print
• 1 (5") A square.
• 4 each of patterns B, C, and D.
From each dark print
• 4 of Pattern E.

continued

Quilt by Rebecca Rohrkaste of Berkeley, California

Block Assembly

1. For each block, select 4 sets of matching C and D pieces, 1 A square, 4 Bs, and 4 E pieces. B and E pieces can match or not, as you prefer.
2. Sew 1 C/D set to each B piece (Block Assembly Diagram). Press seam allowances away from B.
3. Start with any B/C/D unit. Match wide (D) end of unit with A square, with A and B right sides facing. Stitch a partial seam, stopping about half-way down B.
4. Working counter-clockwise around block, add remaining B/C/D units to A square.
5. After last unit is sewn, complete first unit's seam. Press seam allowances toward A.
6. Add E pieces to corners to complete block. Press seam allowances toward Es.
7. Make 30 blocks.

Quilt Assembly

1. Referring to photo, lay out blocks in 6 horizontal rows, with 5 blocks in each row.
2. When satisfied with block placement, join blocks in each row.
3. Join rows.

Quilting and Finishing

1. Mark quilting designs on quilt top as desired. Quilt shown is quilted in-the-ditch.
2. Layer backing, batting, and quilt top. Baste. Quilt as desired.
3. Make 7½ yards of straight-grain or bias binding. Bind quilt edges.

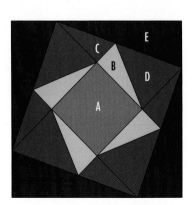

Block Assembly Diagram

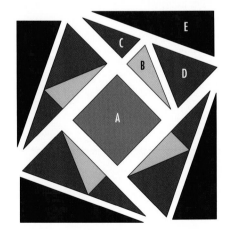

Tipped Star Block*—Make 30.
* Quilt historians identify this block as Delaware Cross Patch, first published as a Nancy Cabot pattern in the 1930s.

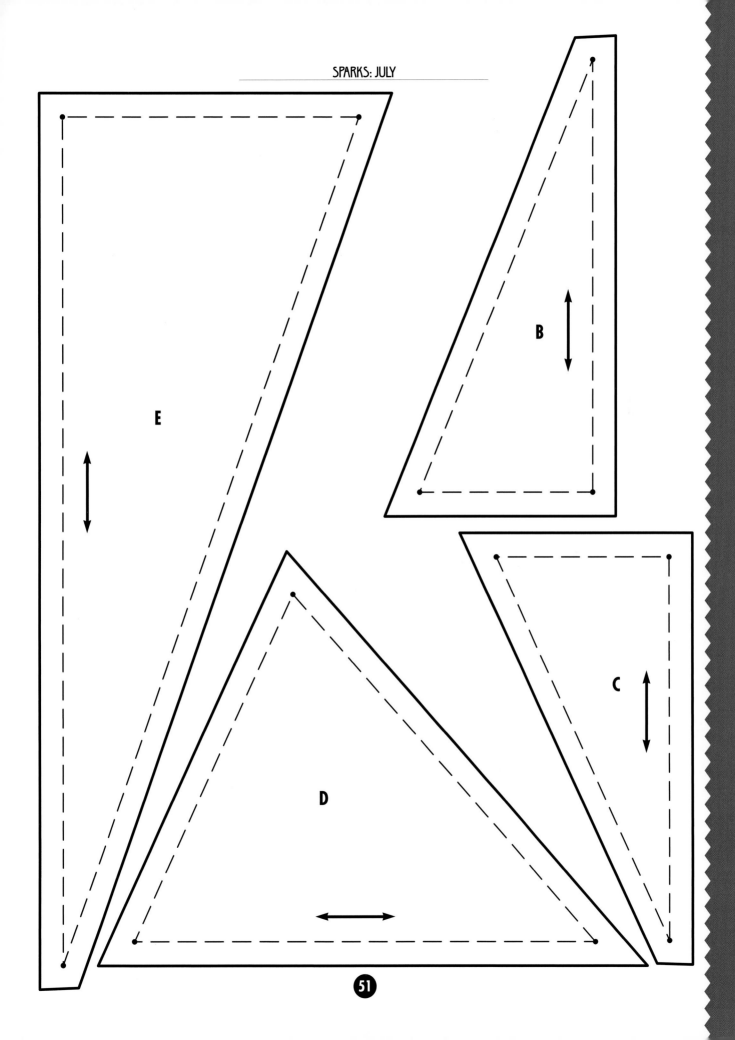

DRESDEN ON THE HALF SHELL

Quilt by Bette Lee Collins of Red Bluff, California

A friend gave Bette Lee Collins a stack of 1930s Dresden Plate blocks. Bette appliquéd the yellow centers and created this scrappy setting and border with authentic 1930s fabrics. "The half-shell (or clam-shell) quilting seemed to give the quilt a continuous motion that I liked," says Bette. She combined the block name and quilting pattern name to dub her quilt "Dresden on the Half Shell."

Finished Size

Quilt: 70" x 87"
Blocks: 12 (15" x 15")

Materials

24 fat quarters (18" x 22") assorted prints for blocks and borders (approximately 5 yards total)
⅛ yard green for stems
¼ yard yellow for sashing squares and appliqué
4¾ yards white for background
¾ yard binding fabric
5½ yards backing fabric
¼"-wide bias pressing bars (optional)

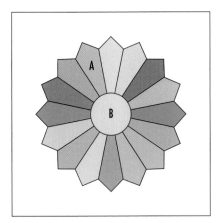

Dresden Plate Block—Make 12.

Cutting

Cut all strips cross-grain except as noted. Make templates for patterns A and B, leaf, small circle, small posy, medium posy, and large posy on page 55.
From assorted prints
- 192 As.
- 136 (2½" x 4¼") C rectangles for sashing and borders.
- 74 (2½" x 4½") D rectangles. Be sure to keep C and D rectangles separate. You might put each group in a labelled zip-top plastic bag until needed.
- 128 leaves.
- 4 large posies.
- 22 medium posies.
- 18 small posies.
From green plaid
- 4 (⅞"-wide) strips. Fold strips in thirds so they are approximately ¼"-wide and press (use bias bars for pressing, if desired). Cut strips into 14 (9"-long) stems.
From yellow
- 12 Bs.
- 22 small circles for posy centers.
- 6 (2½") sashing squares.
From white
- 2 (7" x 72") lengthwise strips for side borders and 2 (7" x 68") lengthwise strips for top and bottom borders.
- 12 (15½") background squares.

Block Assembly

1. Join 16 A pieces to make a circle. Baste under ¼" seam allowance around outer edge.
2. Fold and crease background squares in half horizontally, vertically, and diagonally to make appliqué guidelines. Pin pieced circle on background square, aligning points of A pieces with creased guidelines.
3. Baste under ¼" seam allowance around edges of B piece. Center B on A circle. Appliqué A and B to background. Make 12 blocks (Dresden Plate Block Diagram).
4. Turn block over. Carefully trim background fabric behind A and B, leaving ¼" seam allowance.

Quilt Assembly

1. Join 4 C pieces to make a sashing strip. Make 17 sashing strips.
2. Lay out 4 horizontal rows with 3 blocks and 2 sashing strips in each row (Quilt Assembly Diagram). Join units in each row. Press seam allowances toward blocks.
3. Join 3 sashing strips and 2 yellow squares to make each sashing row as shown. Make 3 sashing rows.
4. Join block rows and sashing rows to complete quilt center.

continued

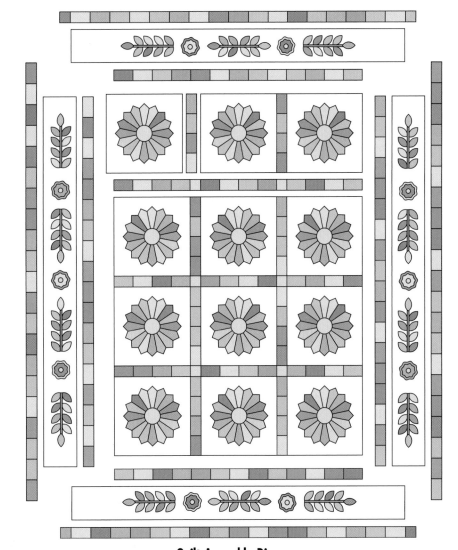

Quilt Assembly Diagram

Borders

1. For top inner borner, join 12 C pieces and 1 D piece. Join to top edge of quilt, easing to fit as needed. Repeat for bottom border.

2. For each side border, join 8 C pieces and 10 Ds. Sew borders to quilt sides, easing to fit as needed.

3. Measure length of quilt through center of quilt top. Trim longer white border strips to match length. Sew these to quilt sides, easing to fit. Press seam allowances toward borders. Measure width of quilt; then trim remaining white strips to match width. Sew borders to top and bottom edges of quilt.

4. At each border corner, appliqué a large posy (Border Corner Diagram). Appliqué a medium posy on top; then add a small circle.

5. Appliqué medium posies at sides of each large posy as shown. Add a small posy on top of each medium posy; then add a small circle.

Border Corner Diagram

6. Center remaining medium posies on white borders in line with sashing strips (Quilt Assembly Diagram). Appliqué posies in place; then add small posies and small circles on each.

7. Center stems and leaves between medium posies as shown. Note different position of leaves at center top and center bottom. When satisfied with placement, appliqué pieces to borders.

8. For each side border, join 4 C pieces and 17 D pieces. Sew borders to quilt sides, easing to fit.

9. For top bottom, join 10 C pieces and 9 Ds. Center border at top edge and trim ends to match quilt width. Sew border to top edge of quilt. Repeat for bottom border.

Quilting and Finishing

1. Mark quilting designs on quilt top as desired. Quilt shown is outline-quilted in fans and around appliqué. Blocks are filled with a clamshell design. Appliquéd border is outline-quilted with echo quilting around posies. Outer border has a scallop pattern in each rectangle.

2. Layer backing, batting, and quilt top. Baste. Quilt as desired.

3. Make 9 yards of straight-grain binding. Bind quilt edges.

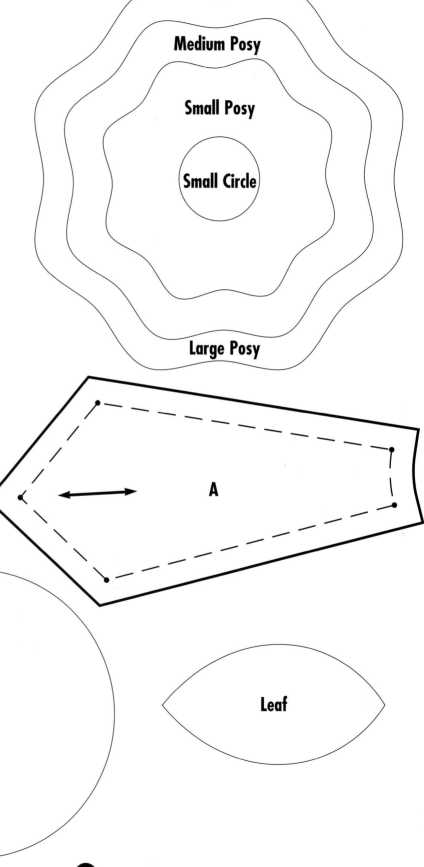

Medium Posy

Small Posy

Small Circle

Large Posy

A

B

Leaf

FUNKY CHICKEN

Quilt by Freddy Moran of Orinda, California

The class assignment was to create an original design based on a natural theme. Much to Freddy Moran's surprise, her imagination hatched this funny chicken block. "I've no idea how I arrived at this," Freddy says, "but I love the whimsy of it." The blocks make a notable border for a bouquet of Painted Daisy blocks, which Freddy found in Ruth McDowell's book, *Symmetry*. When she saw the pattern, Freddy says, "I knew my chickens had found a place to roost."

Finished Size

Quilt: 80" x 86"
Blocks:
40 (5" x 8") chicken blocks
 9 (14" x 14") Painted Daisy blocks
28 (6⅛" x 7⅞") daisy quarter-blocks

Materials

2⅜ yards white fabric for border
¾ yard *each* 4 white or beige prints
¾ yard red stripe fabric*
⅝ yard red for chicken combs
¼ yard orange for beak
¼ yard *each* 16 plaids for daisies
¼ yard *each* 2 brown prints
¼ yard *each* 10 prints for chicken backgrounds
¼ yard black-on-white print
20 (4" x 15") scraps for chickens
10 (6") squares gold for chicken feet
⅞ yard binding fabric
2⅝ yards 90"-wide backing fabric
* *Note:* Yardage is for pieced borders. To cut lengthwise borders, you need 2¼ yards.

Cutting

Cut strips cross-grain except as noted. Make templates for patterns A–J on pages 60 and 61. Cutting and piecing instructions for other pieces are for rotary cutting and quick piecing. Cut pieces in order listed to get best use of yardage.

From white fabric
• 4 (4¼" x 84") border strips. Use remainder for piecing, if desired.

From each white/beige print
• 16 of Pattern A.
• 16 of Pattern C.
• 16 of Pattern D.
• 16 of Pattern G.
• 16 of Pattern I.
• 16 of Pattern F.

From red
• 1 (12"-wide) strip. From this and remaining fabric, cut 10 (6" x 12") pieces for chicken comb triangle-squares.

From orange
• 20 (2⅝") squares. Cut squares in half diagonally to get 40 P triangles.

From each plaid
• 4 of Pattern B.
• 4 of Pattern E.
• 4 of Pattern H.

From brown print 1
• 64 of Pattern J.

From brown print 2
• 25 (2½") L squares.

From each chicken background fabric (makes 4 blocks)
• 1 (6" x 12") piece for comb N triangle-squares.
• 1 (6") square for feet N triangle-squares.
• 2 (2⅝") squares. Cut squares in half diagonally to get 4 P triangles, 1 for each block.
• 8 (1½" x 5½") O pieces, 2 for each block.
• 12 (1½") Q squares, 3 for each block.
• 4 (1½") squares for N diagonal-corners, 1 for each block.
• 2 (1½" x 8½") strips for border spacers (cut from only 4 fabrics to get a total of 8).

From black-on-white print
• 16 (2½" x 6⅜") K pieces.

From each chicken scrap (makes 2 blocks)
• 2 (3½" x 4½") M pieces, 1 for each block.
• 2 (2½") L squares, 1 for each block.

Painted Daisy Block Assembly

1. For each quarter-block unit, select 1 each of B, E, and H from same fabric (Diagram A). Choose 1 each of pieces A, C, D, F, G, and I, mixing background fabrics as desired.
2. Working in alphabetical order, join pieces in 3 sections as shown. Join sections. Set-in a J piece to complete quarter-block unit. Make 4 identical quarter-

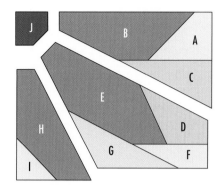

Diagram A

block units for each daisy, a total of 64 units (16 sets of 4).
3. Sew brown L squares to 1 end of each K strip.
4. Lay out units in rows, matching fabrics and rotating units to form daisies (Quilt Assembly Diagram).

continued

Quilt Assembly Diagram

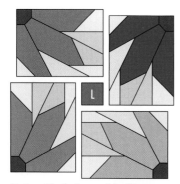

Daisy Block Assembly Diagram

5. Sew a K/L unit to 5 quarter-blocks in top row as shown. Press seam allowances toward K/L. Then join units in top row, being sure to check position against diagram. Repeat for bottom row.

6. For second row, join a K/L unit to quarter-blocks at each end as shown; then join 2 quarter-blocks to make each end unit.

7. Each Painted Daisy block has 4 quarter-blocks of a different fabric sewn around an L square. To begin, stitch L to bottom of top left unit (Daisy Block Assembly Diagram), matching corners as shown, but do not complete seam—stop sewing about half-way down length of L. Add top right unit, stitching a complete seam. Add bottom right unit in same manner; then join bottom left unit. When all 4 units are sewn to L, complete first unit seam to edge of block.

8. Make 8 more daisy blocks in same manner. Return each completed block to quilt layout to check for correct placement and alignment of matching fabrics in adjacent blocks.

9. When blocks are complete, join blocks and end units in each row.

Chicken Block Assembly

1. On wrong side of each 6" x 12" background piece, draw a 2-square by 5-square grid of 1⅞" squares, leaving a 1" margin on all sides (Diagram B). Draw diagonal lines through each square as shown.

2. Match each marked piece with a 6" x 12" piece of red fabric, right sides facing. Stitch ¼" seam on both sides of diagonal lines. (Red line on diagram indicates first continuous stitching path, blue line shows second path.) Press.

3. Cut on all drawn lines to get 20 comb triangle-squares, 5 for each of 4 blocks.

4. On wrong side of each 6" square of background fabric, draw a 2-square by 2-square grid of 1⅞" squares (Diagram C). Draw diagonal lines through each square as shown. Match each marked piece with a 6" square of gold fabric, right sides facing. Stitch grid as before. Press. Cut on drawn lines to get 8 triangle-squares for feet, 2 for each of 4 blocks.

5. For each block, select 1 L/M set and 1 orange P triangle. Then choose 5 comb triangle-squares, 2 feet triangle-squares, 1 P triangle, 2 O strips, 3 Q squares, and 1 N diagonal-corner square, all with same background fabric.

6. See page 11 for tips on diagonal-corner quick-piecing technique. Follow those instructions to sew N square to 1 corner of M (Chicken Block Assembly Diagram).

7. Join P triangles as shown. Stitch P square to 1 side of L. Join 2 comb triangle-squares as shown

and join to opposite side of L. Press seam allowances toward L. (*Note:* On quilt shown, some combs are turned this way and that for added charm.)

8. Sew 3 comb triangle-squares and 2 Qs in a row as shown. Press seam allowances toward Qs. Stitch row to top of head unit.

9. Join 1 Q and 2 feet triangle-squares in a row. Sew feet to bottom of M. Press seam allowances toward M. Then sew O strips to unit sides as shown. Press seam allowances toward Os.

10. Join head and body units to complete block.

11. Make 40 chicken blocks.

Borders

1. Cut 16 (1½"-wide) strips from red stripe. Join pairs of strips end-to-end to assemble borders.

2. For each side border, select 7 chicken blocks, including 1 block in each row that matches a pair of spacer strips. Sew spacers to top and bottom edges of matching block, trimming strips to fit. Press seam allowances toward spacers.

3. Join 7 blocks in a vertical row (Quilt Assembly Diagram), placing spacer block in middle of row.

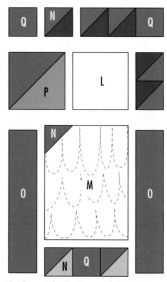

Chicken Block Assembly Diagram

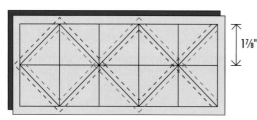

Diagram B

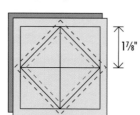

Diagram C

4. Matching centers, sew a red border strip to inside edge of each chicken row. Trim excess fabric from border ends. (Save scraps for top and bottom borders.) Sew borders to quilt sides, easing to fit as needed.

5. For top border, select 13 chicken blocks, including 1 with matching spacer strips. Sew spacers to both sides of block. Then join 11 blocks in a horizontal row, with spacer block at center (Quilt Assembly Diagram). From red border scraps, cut 2 (1½" x 8½") pieces and sew 1 piece to each end of row. Join remaining chicken blocks to row ends as shown.

6. Matching centers, sew a red border strip to inside edge of chicken row. Trim excess fabric from ends of border. Sew border to top edge of quilt, easing to fit as needed.

7. Repeat steps 5 and 6 for bottom border.

8. Sew 2 red borders to quilt sides. Trim excess fabric. Join red borders to top and bottom edges of quilt in same manner.

9. Measure length of quilt through middle of quilt top. Trim 2 white borders to this measurement. Sew border strips to quilt sides, easing to fit as needed. Measure width of quilt through middle, including side borders. Trim remaining strips to fit and stitch to top and bottom edges.

Quilting and Finishing

1. Mark quilt top with desired quilting design. On quilt shown, a hexagon pattern is quilted over daisies to look like chicken wire. Chicken blocks have quilted feathers, and more chickens are quilted in white borders. Patterns for hexagon and chicken designs are on page 61. For feathers, mark irregular scallops to look like feathers.

2. Layer backing, batting, and quilt top. Baste. Quilt chicken blocks in-the-ditch. Quilt remainder of quilt as marked or as desired.

3. Make 9½ yards of continuous bias or straight grain binding. Bind quilt edges.

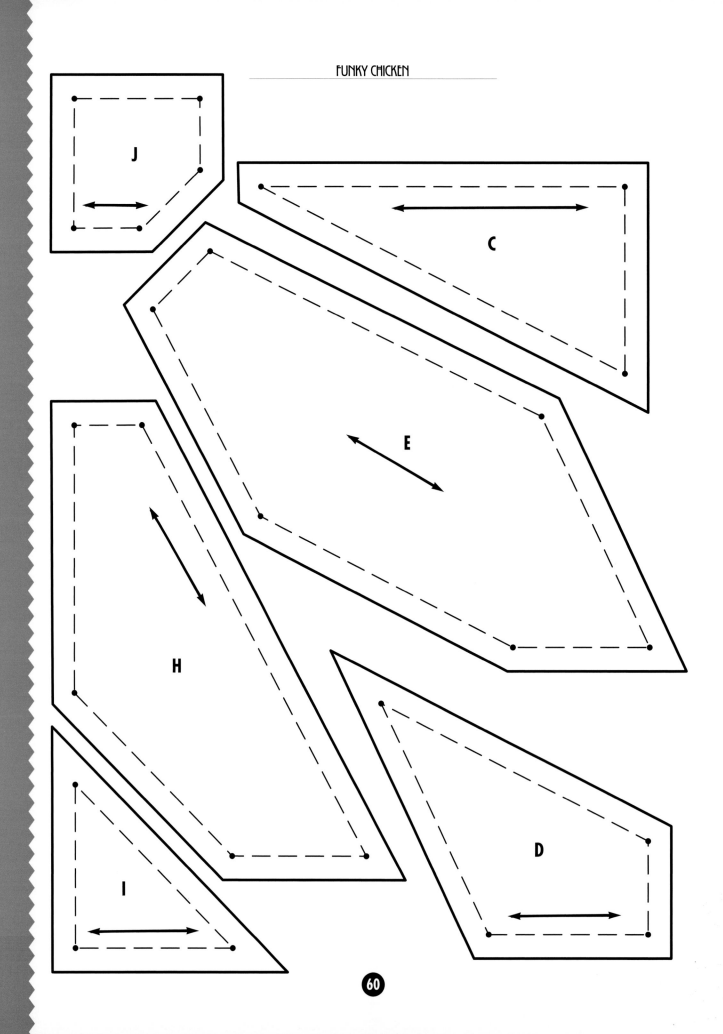

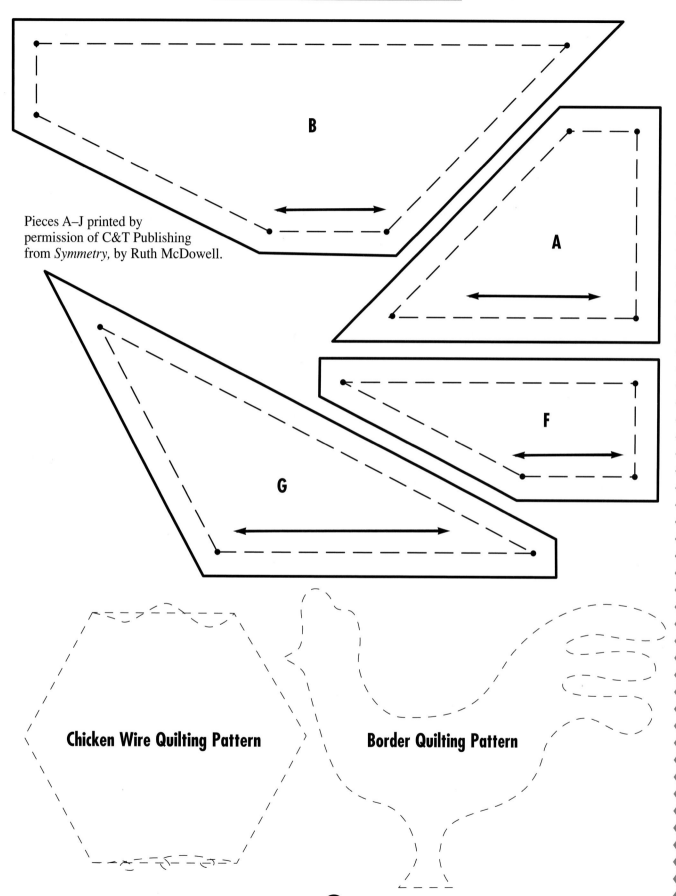

Pieces A–J printed by permission of C&T Publishing from *Symmetry,* by Ruth McDowell.

B

A

F

G

Chicken Wire Quilting Pattern

Border Quilting Pattern

STREAK OF LIGHTNING

Quilt by Rhonda Richards of Birmingham, Alabama;
machine-quilted by New Traditions of Birmingham, Alabama

Believe it or not, you don't cut any triangles to make this quilt. Rhonda Richards used a neat quick-piecing technique developed by Sally Schneider. It's an easy way to turn out a lot of blocks in no time. Rhonda made her quilt with cheery Christmas fabrics, but you can use any theme or color scheme to piece this striking design.

Finished Size
Quilt: 73" x 78"
Blocks: 132 (4" x 4")

Materials
11 fat quarters (18" x 22") dark prints
1⅜ yards white or muslin
½ yard dark border fabric
¾ yard print border fabric
2⅛ yards outer border fabric
  (includes binding)*
4½ yards backing fabric
Template plastic
*Excess fabric can replace 1 or more
fat quarters, if desired.

Cutting

Instructions are for rotary cutting and quick piecing. Cut strips cross-grain except as noted.

From outer border fabric
• 4 (5" x 76") lengthwise strips.
• 5 (2½" x 76") strips for binding. Use remaining fabric for piecing, if desired.

From each dark fat quarter
• 2 (3" x 18") strips. From these, cut 12 (3") squares to get a total of 132 A squares.
• 2 (6½" x 18") strips. From these, cut 6 (5½" x 6½") C pieces to get a total of 66 Cs.

From white
• 10 (4"-wide) strips. From these, cut 132 (3" x 4") B pieces.

Block Assembly

1. Sew each A square to 1 end of each B piece.

2. Join A/B units in pairs, placing A squares at opposite ends as shown.

3. Turn block over. Clip seam allowance between dark squares. Then press seam allowances in opposite directions.

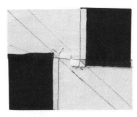

4. Make template of triangle pattern (page 64), drawing square within triangle as shown. With template on *wrong* side of block, align lines of square with square A. Mark diagonal line with pencil. Move template to opposite corner of block and draw another diagonal line.

5. Match each marked block with a 5½" x 6½" C piece, right sides facing. Stitch on both drawn lines. Cut block in half between sewn lines to get 2 finished blocks.

6. Open each block and press seam allowance toward C triangle.
7. Make 132 blocks.

Quilt Assembly

1. Refer to photo to lay out blocks in 11 horizontal rows with 12 blocks in each row. Turn blocks as needed to achieve zigzag design.
2. When satisfied with placement, join blocks in each row.
3. Join rows.

Borders

1. From dark fabric for first border, cut 8 (2"-wide) strips. Join 2 strips end-to-end to make a border for each edge of quilt.
2. Measure width of quilt through middle of quilt top. Trim 2 border strips to this measurement. Stitch border strips to top and bottom edges of quilt, easing to fit as necessary.
3. Measure length of quilt through middle of quilt top, including top and bottom borders. Trim remaining border strips to match length. Stitch border strips to quilt sides.
4. From print border fabric, cut 8 (3"-wide) strips. Join 2 strips end-to-end to make each border strip. Repeat steps 2 and 3 to add print borders to edges of quilt.
5. Add outer border strips in same manner.

Quilting and Finishing

1. Mark quilt top with desired quilting design. Quilt shown is commercially machine-quilted.
2. Layer backing, batting, and quilt top. Baste. Quilt as desired.
3. Make 8⅝ yards of straight-grain binding from reserved border fabric. Bind quilt edges.

continued

Other Sets: You can turn this versatile block to create different sets. Here are just a few examples. Kelly Davis made the Barn Raising set (top right) with 196 blocks, offsetting with red and green diagonal rows in opposite corners. The Jewel Box set, made by Emily Parrish, has 180 blocks. These quilts were made in a class led by Marge LaBenne of Tucker, Georgia.

Quick-Piecing Pattern

WASATCH MEMORIES

Quilt by Bobbi Finley of San Jose, California

When she moved to California, Bobbi Finley missed the change of seasons that she used to love. So when autumn came without the annual show of colorful leaves, Bobbi decided to make an autumn leaf quilt. From her collection of glowing leaf fabrics, Bobbi pieced an original leaf block based on the traditional Drunkard's Path. The finished quilt reminds her of happy times at her former home near the Wasatch Mountains of Utah.

Finished Size

Quilt: 64" x 64"
Blocks: 64 (6" x 6")

Materials

64 (10") squares leaf prints
2½ yards dark brown
¾ yard light brown print for vine
¾ yard gold print for vine leaves
¾ yard rust print for narrow borders
¾ yard binding fabric
4 yards backing fabric

continued

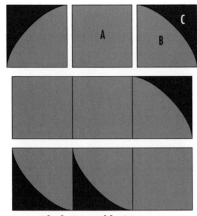

Block Assembly Diagram

Cutting

Make templates of patterns on page 67. Cut all strips cross-grain except as noted. Cut pieces in order listed to get best use of yardage.
From each leaf print
• 4 (2½") A squares.
• 5 of Pattern B.
From dark brown
• 2 (6½" x 64") lengthwise border strips.
• 2 (6½" x 52") lengthwise border strips.
• 320 of Pattern C.
From gold print
• 27 of Pattern F.
• 21 of Pattern E.
• 20 of Pattern D.
From rust print
• 16 (1½"-wide) strips.

Block Assembly

1. For each block, select a set of 4 A pieces and 5 Bs.
2. Sew a brown C piece to each B.
3. Join units in a row as shown (Block Assembly Diagram). Join rows to complete block.
4. Make 64 blocks.

Quilt Assembly

1. Lay out blocks in 8 horizontal rows with 8 blocks in each row. Referring to photo, turn blocks in top 4 rows up and blocks in bottom 4 rows down.
2. When satisfied with block placement, join blocks in each row. Then join rows.

Borders

1. Join 2 rust print strips end-to-end to make each border strip. Sew 2 border strips to quilt sides; then trim excess fabric from strip. Join 2 border strips to top and bottom edges of quilt. Press seam allowances toward borders.
2. Sew longer dark brown strips to quilt sides; then sew remaining strips to top and bottom edges.
3. Repeat Step 1 to join outer rust print border strips to quilt.
4. See page 143 for instructions on making continuous bias. From light brown print, make 7½ yards of 1¼"-wide continuous bias. Fold bias in thirds to make a ⅜"-wide vine; press.
5. From continuous bias strip, cut 27 (3"-long) stems, 21 (3¾"-long) stems, and 20 (4½"-long) stems. Set stems aside.

6. Referring to photo, pin remaining length of bias to brown border for vine. Pin leaves and stems in place, matching 3"-long stems with F leaves, 3¾"-long stems with Es, and 4½"-long stems with Ds.
7. When satisfied with placement, appliqué leaves, stems, and vine in place.

Quilting and Finishing

1. Mark quilt top with desired quilting designs. Quilt shown is outline-quilted with veins quilted in pieced leaves.
2. Layer backing, batting, and quilt top. Baste. Quilt as desired.
3. Make 7¼ yards of continuous bias or straight-grain binding. Bind quilt edges.

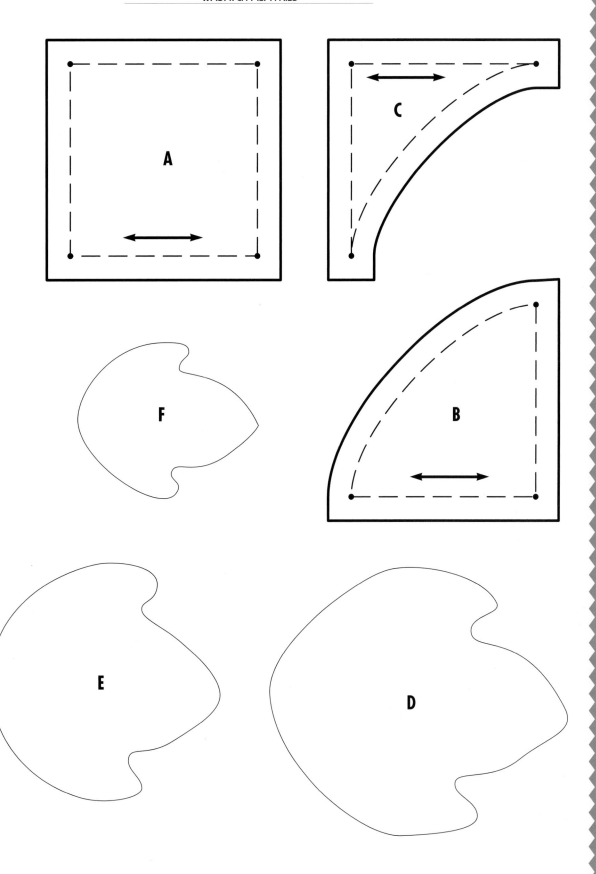

ROSEMARY'S BUTTERFLIES

Quilt by Rosemary Youngs of Walker, Michigan

Rosemary Youngs collected 1930s vintage fabrics for this quilt at an estate sale. The fabrics remind Rosemary of "quilts my grandmothers would have made if they'd been quilters." Rosemary began her block design with a traditional tulip pattern in the center and added butterflies for balance. *Butterflies* is Rosemary's first appliqué quilt, made for daughter, Amy. "I know she will always cherish and love it," Rosemary says, "and that's what quilts are for!"

Finished Size

Quilt: 77" x 77"
Blocks: 9 (19" x 19")

Materials

36 (4½" x 6½") pastel print scraps
5⅝ yards white (includes binding)
1¼ yards green
⅛ yard pink
⅛ yard blue
4¾ yards backing
¼"-wide bias pressing bar (optional)
Freezer paper

Cutting

Cut all strips cross-grain except as noted. Make templates of patterns A–G on page 71. Cut pieces in order listed to get best use of yardage.

From each pastel scrap
• 1 of Pattern A.

From white
• 2 (10½" x 80") and 2 (10½" x 60") lengthwise border strips.
• 9 (19½") squares.
• 2 (19") squares for binding.

From green
• 1 (15") square for bias vines.
• 7 (2"-wide) strips. From these, cut 68 of Pattern D, 13 of Pattern E, and 16 of Pattern G.
• 44 of Pattern C.

From pink
• 2 (2¼"-wide) strips. From these, cut 20 of Pattern B and 8 of Pattern F.

From blue
• 2 (2¼"-wide) strips. From these, cut 24 of Pattern B and 8 of Pattern F.

Block Assembly

1. Cut a 14" square of freezer paper. Fold paper in quarters. Use ruler and pencil to draw a quarter-circle with a 7" radius on paper. Cut on drawn line through all 4 layers. Unfold to get a pattern for a 14"-diameter circle.
2. Fold each white fabric square into quarters horizontally, vertically, and diagonally (Diagram A). Crease folds for placement guidelines.
3. Center circle pattern on fabric. Lightly trace perimeter of circle on fabric. Remove pattern. Mark a second circle ¼" outside first. Mark all squares in same manner.
4. Position 1 E at center of each block. Then place 4 Cs and 4 Ds, aligning pieces with creased placement guides (¼ Block Appliqué Placement Diagram). Insert 4 blue Bs under C pieces (or 4 pink Bs in 4 blocks). Align scrap butterflies on marked circles at diagonal placement lines as shown.

Butterflies Block—Make 9.

5. When satisfied with placement of pieces on each block, appliqué pieces in alphabetical order.
6. Make 5 blocks with blue B pieces and 4 blocks with pink B pieces.

Quilt Assembly

1. Referring to photo on page 70, lay out blocks in 3 horizontal rows of 3 blocks each. Alternate blocks with blue B pieces and pink Bs as shown.

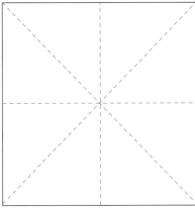

Diagram A

2. Join blocks in each row.
3. Join rows.

Borders

1. From green square, cut 16 (¾"-wide) bias strips. Trim 8 strips to 6¼" long and 8 strips to 9" long. Fold and press each strip in thirds (use bias pressing bar, if desired) to get ¼"-wide vine pieces.

continued

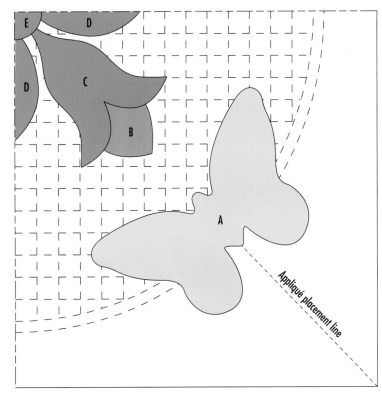

¼ Block Appliqué Placement Diagram

2. Fold each border strip in half to find center. Position an E piece on each border at this point, 2" from 1 long edge. Position Cs on both sides of E as shown (½ *Border Appliqué Placement Diagram*). Place short vine strips; then longer strips, adding Ds, Gs, and Fs as shown.

3. When satisified with placement of appliqué pieces, stitch vines in place. Then appliqué remaining pieces in alphabetical order.

4. Measure width of quilt through middle of quilt top. Trim 2 (60") border strips to this measurement, measuring from center of border strip. Stitch borders to top and bottom edges of quilt, easing to fit as needed.

5. Measure length of quilt through middle of quilt top. Trim remaining borders to this length, measuring from center of border strip. Sew border strips to quilt sides.

Quilting and Finishing

1. Mark quilt top with desired quilting design. Quilt shown is hand-quilted with a ½" cross-hatch pattern quilted inside marked circles. Pattern for plume quilted in block corners is on page 71. Borders are quilted in vertical lines spaced ½" apart.

2. Layer backing, batting, and quilt top. Baste. Outline-quilt around all appliqué pieces. Quilt circles on marked lines. Add additional quilting as marked or as desired.

3. Make 8¾ yards of continuous bias or straight-grain binding. Bind quilt edges.

Reverse along this line.

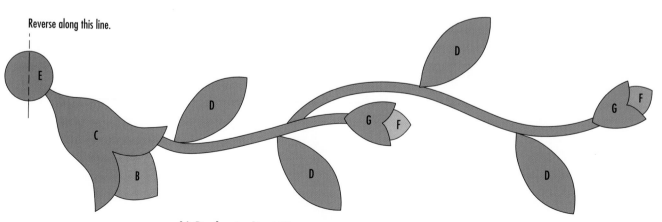

½ Border Appliqué Placement Diagram (40% of actual size)

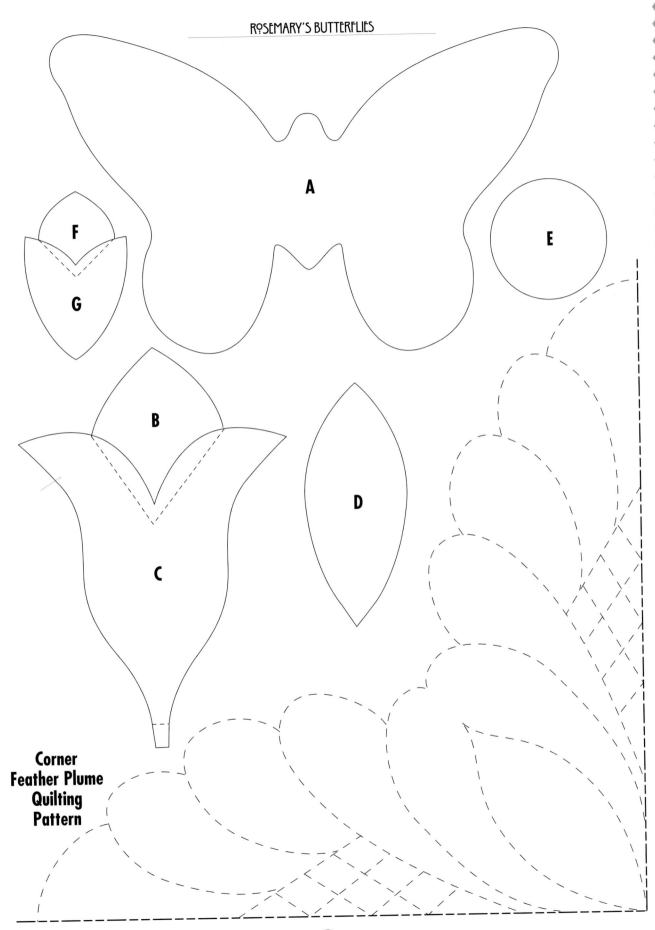

**Corner
Feather Plume
Quilting
Pattern**

ODD FELLOWS MARCH

Quilt by Susan Marie Stewart of Buena Vista, Colorado

Patterns within patterns emerge when these blocks come together. Big stars and squares-within-squares appear that aren't suggested when you see the original block. (The block is also known as Crosses and Losses or Double X.) Susan Stewart used a plethora of plaids to make these earth-tone blocks, surrounded by a flock of flying geese units in the borders. The quilt is just as fun in pastels or primary colors.

Finished Size
Quilt: 82½" x 90½"
Blocks: 56 (8" x 8")

Materials
5½ yards muslin
1¾ yards 60"-wide red plaid for bias inner border (or 1½ yards 45"-wide for pieced border)
½ yard green for middle border
2⅜ yards brown check for outer border
25 (12" x 13") dark plaids for blocks
8 (7" x 13") dark plaids for Goose Chase border
4 (4½") red squares for inner border corners
⅞ yard brown plaid for outer border corners and binding
2¾ yards 90"-wide backing fabric
8 buttons (optional)

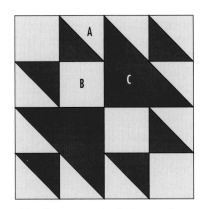

Odd Fellows March Block—Make 56.

Cutting

Instructions are for rotary cutting and quick piecing. Cut all strips cross-grain except as noted. Cut pieces in order listed to get best use of yardage.

From muslin

- 7 (13"-wide) strips. From these, cut 38 (7" x 13") pieces for block triangle-squares and pieced border.
- 15 (2⅞"-wide) strips. From these, cut 112 (2⅞") squares. Cut squares in half diagonally to get 224 A triangles (4 for each block).
- 13 (2½"-wide) strips. From these and scrap, cut 224 (2½") B squares (4 for each block).

From red plaid

- 4 (4½" x 76") bias strips from corner to corner for first border.
- 1 (12" x 13") piece for blocks.
- 1 (7" x 13") for border.

From brown check

- 4 (4½" x 85") lengthwise strips for outer border.
- 2 (12" x 13") pieces for blocks.
- 1 (7" x 13") for border.

From each 12" x 13" plaid (including red and brown pieces above)

- 1 (7" x 13") piece for block triangle-squares.
- 2 (4⅞") squares. Cut each square in half diagonally to get 4 C triangles (2 for each block).

From brown plaid

- 1 (30") square for binding.
- 4 (4½") squares for outer border corners.

Block Assembly

1. On wrong side of a 7" x 13" muslin piece, draw a 2-square by 4-square grid of 2⅞" squares, leaving a 1" margin on all sides (Diagram A). Draw diagonal lines through each square as shown.

2. Match marked muslin piece with a 7" x 13" plaid piece, right sides facing. Stitch ¼" seam on both sides of diagonal lines. (Blue line on diagram indicates first continuous stitching path, red line shows second path.) Press.

3. Cut on all drawn lines to get 16 triangle-squares.

4. Stitch 28 triangle-square grids to get 56 sets of 6 triangle-squares for each block. Set aside 112 remaining triangle-squares for Goose Chase border.

5. For each block, select 6 triangle-squares and 2 C triangles of same fabric, as well as 4 A triangles and B squares.

6. Sew an A triangle to both dark sides of 1 triangle-square (Diagram B). Press seam allowances toward A triangles. Add C triangle to complete A/C unit. Make 2 A/C units for each block.

7. Sew B squares to dark sides of each remaining triangle-square (Diagram C). Press seam allowances toward Bs. Join 2 of these units to complete B unit. Make 2 B units for each block.

8. Join A/C units and B units in 2 rows (Block Assembly Diagram). Join rows to complete block.

9. Make 56 blocks.

continued

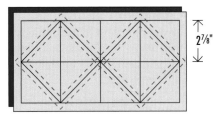

Diagram A

Diagram B

Diagram C

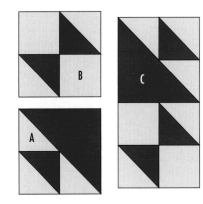

Block Assembly Diagram

Quilt Assembly

1. Lay out blocks in 8 horizontal rows, with 7 blocks in each row. Turn adjacent blocks as shown (Quilt Assembly Diagram).
2. When satisfied with block placement, join blocks in each row.
3. Join rows.

Borders

1. Center a red plaid border on each side of quilt and stitch. Miter corners. Press seam allowances toward borders.
2. Mark triangle-square grid on 10 remaining 7" x 13" muslin pieces. Pair each marked piece with a plaid piece and stitch grids as before to get 160 more triangle-squares. With reserved units, you should have 272.
3. Join triangle-squares in pairs to make 136 Goose Chase units (Diagram D).

Diagram D

4. Join 36 units in row for each side border (Quilt Assembly Diagram). Sew borders to quilt sides, easing to fit as needed.
5. For top and bottom borders, join remaining units in 2 (32-unit) rows. Add a 4½" red plaid square to each end of both strips. Sew borders to top and bottom edges of quilt, easing to fit as needed.
6. Cut 8 (1¾"-wide) strips of green fabric. Join 2 strips end-to-end for each border. Center a border on each edge of quilt and stitch. Miter border corners.
7. Measure length of quilt though middle of quilt top. Trim 2 brown check borders to match length. Sew borders to quilt sides, easing to fit as needed.
8. Measure width of quilt through middle of quilt top. Trim remaining brown check borders to match width. Stitch borders to top and bottom edges of quilt.

Quilt Assembly Diagram

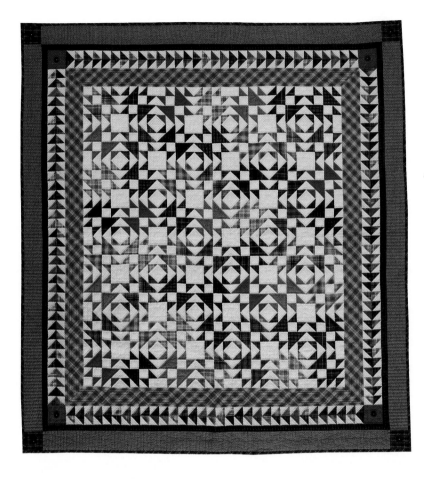

Celtic Chain Quilting Pattern

Quilting and Finishing

1. Mark quilt top with desired quilt-ing design. On quilt shown, blocks and Goose Chase border are outline-quilted, with echo quilting in muslin triangles. A Variable Star is quilted in B squares where 4 blocks meet and in border corner squares. Pattern for Celtic Chain quilted in bias plaid border is at right.
2. Layer backing, batting, and quilt top. Baste. Quilt as desired.
3. Make 10 yards of continuous bias or straight-grain binding. Bind quilt edges.
4. Add buttons to border corners.

PINK LEMONADE

Quilt by Shelby Sawyer Morris of Cartersville, Georgia

Lemonade is refreshing on hot summer days in the South, where Shelby Morris lives. Inspired by the floral border fabric, Shelby quick-pieced Shoo-fly blocks in pastel colors that reminded her of sweet summertime pleasures.

Finished Sizes
Quilt: 64" x 80"
Blocks: 48 (6" x 6")

Materials
½ yard *each* 5 light prints
¼ yard *each* 7 dark prints
¼ yard *each* 2 pink prints for frames
¾ yard medium pink floral print for frames and inner border
1½ yards dark blue print for frames, middle border, and binding
2½ yards yellow floral border fabric
2 yards 90"-wide backing fabric

Cutting

Instructions are for rotary cutting and quick piecing. Cut all strips cross-grain except as noted. Cut pieces in order listed to get best use of yardage.

From light prints

- 7 (2⅞"-wide) strips. From these, cut 96 (2⅞") squares. Cut squares in half diagonally to get 192 A triangles, 4 for each block.
- 12 (2½"-wide) strips. From these, cut 192 (2½") B squares, 4 for each block.
- 16 (1½"-wide) strips (3 of each print). From these, cut 40 (8½"-long) strips and 40 (6½"-long) strips for 20 frames, 4 matching strips for each block.

From dark prints

- 7 (2⅞"-wide) strips. From these, cut 96 (2⅞") squares. Cut squares in half diagonally to get 192 A triangles, 4 for each block.
- 7 (2½"-wide) strips. From these, cut 48 (2½") B squares, 1 for each block center.

From medium pink floral print

- 6 (2½"-wide) strips for inner border. Add remaining fabric to pink prints for frames.

From 3 pink prints for frames

- 11 (1½"-wide) strips. From these, cut 28 (8½"-long) strips and 28 (6½"-long) strips for 14 frames, 4 matching strips for each block.

From dark blue print

- 7 (1½"-wide) strips for middle border.
- 11 (1½"-wide) strips. From these, cut 30 (8½"-long) strips and 30 (6½"-long) strips for 15 frames, 4 matching strips for each block.
- 8 (2½"-wide) strips for binding.

From yellow floral

- 4 (5½" x 72") lengthwise strips for outer border.

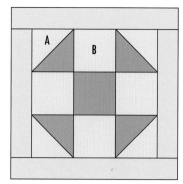

Shoo-Fly Block—Make 48.

Block Assembly

1. For each block, select 4 A triangles and 4 B squares from same light fabric. Then choose 4 A triangles and 1 B square from same dark fabric.
2. Join light and dark triangles to make a triangle-square (Block Assembly Diagram).
3. Arrange triangle-squares and B squares in rows as shown. Join units in each row; then join rows. Press seam allowances toward light fabric Bs.
4. Select a set of 4 frame strips. Sew 6½" strips to block sides. Press seam allowances toward strips. Then add 8½" strips to top and bottom edges to complete block.
5. Make 48 blocks, choosing light and dark combinations at random.

Quilt Assembly

1. Lay out blocks in 8 horizontal rows, with 6 blocks in each row. Rotate blocks so that frame seams won't meet and make a lump (Frame Diagram).
2. When satisfied with block placement, join blocks in each row.
3. Join rows to complete quilt center.
4. Piece pink border strips to make 2 (66"-long) borders and 2 (54"-long) borders.
5. Measure length of quilt through middle of quilt top. Trim longer strips to match quilt length. Stitch borders to quilt sides.

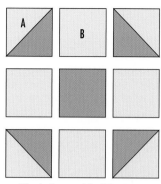

Block Assembly Diagram

6. Measure width of quilt through middle of quilt top. Trim remaining pink strips to match quilt width. Sew borders to top and bottom edges of quilt.
7. Add dark blue middle border and yellow floral outer border in same manner.

Quilting and Finishing

1. Mark quilt top with desired quilting design. Quilt shown is hand-quilted in a Baptist Fan pattern.
2. Layer backing, batting, and quilt top. Baste. Quilt as desired.
3. Join dark blue strips to make 9 yards of continuous straight-grain binding. Bind quilt edges.

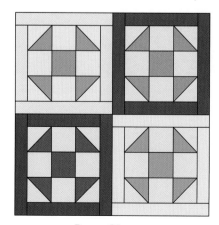

Frame Diagram

NIGHT & NOON STARS

Quilt by Winnie S. Fleming of Houston, Texas

Winnie Fleming likes to give a new look to traditional quilt designs. Using strong colors and a black background, she turns this time-honored block into a dramatic contemporary quilt. The blocks are set so they form a field of bright stars in a dark sky.

Finished Size
Quilt: 51" x 60"
Blocks: 20 (9" x 9")

Materials
14 (8½") squares tone-on-tone prints for blocks and border
10 fat quarters (18" x 22") bright prints
3 yards black (includes binding)
3¼ yards backing fabric

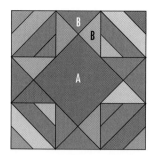

Night & Noon Block—Make 20.

Cutting

Instructions are for rotary cutting and quick piecing. Cut strips cross-grain except as noted. Cut pieces in order listed to get best use of yardage.

From tone-on-tone print squares
- 56 (4¼") squares. Cut each square in quarters diagonally to get 224 B triangles (160 for blocks, 62 for border, and 2 extra).

From each bright print
- 6 (1⅝" x 18") strips for strip sets.
- 2 (4¾") A squares for star centers.
- 6 or 7 (1½") squares to get a total of 66 C squares for border.

From black
- 8 (3½" x 58") lengthwise strips for borders.
- 3 (15" x 18") pieces, cut from length left over from borders. From these, cut 27 (1⅝" x 18") strips for Strip Set 2.
- 1 (25") square for binding.
- 2 (4¼") strips. From these, cut 20 (4¼") squares. Cut each square in quarters diagonally to get 80 B triangles.
- 2 (2¾") strips. From these and scrap, cut 33 (2¾") squares. Cut each square in quarters diagonally to get 132 D triangles for border.

Block Assembly

1. For Strip Set 1, join 2 (1⅝") colored strips. Press seam allowances toward darker fabric. Make 16 of Strip Set 1.
2. Place a strip set on cutting mat. Measure 2¾" from top right corner (reverse directions if you're left-handed). Make a diagonal cut from this point to bottom right

corner (Strip Set 1 Diagram). Measure 5½" along bottom edge. Make second cut from this point to top edge to get first triangle. Continue cutting in this manner to get 5 triangles from each strip set.
3. For Strip Set 2, join each remaining colored strip to a black strip. Make 27 strip sets. Press seam allowances toward black.

4. Cut triangles in same manner as for Strip Set 1, cutting 3 black-bottomed triangles from each strip set (Strip Set 2 Diagram). Discard alternate triangles.
5. Join each black-bottomed triangle to a colored triangle to make each corner unit (Diagram A). Make 80 corner units, 4 for each block.

continued

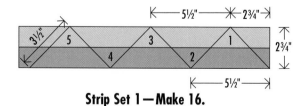

Strip Set 1—Make 16.

Diagram A

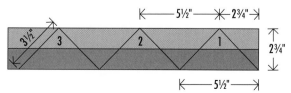

Strip Set 2—Make 27.

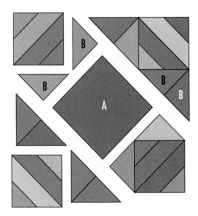

Block Assembly Diagram

Diagram B

Diagram C

6. Sew each black B triangle to a bright B to make a Star Point Unit (Block Assembly Diagram). Make 40 Star Point Units with black triangle on right side and 40 units with black triangle on left. Press seam allowances toward black.

7. For each block, select 4 Star Point units, 1 A square, 4 B triangles, and 4 corner units (Block Assembly Diagram). Join Bs to adjacent sides of 2 corner units as shown; sew these to opposite sides of A.

8. Sew Star Point units to adjacent sides of remaining corner units. Sew these to remaining sides of A to complete block.

9. Make 20 blocks.

Quilt Assembly

1. Lay out blocks in 5 horizontal rows, with 4 blocks in each row (Quilt Assembly Diagram).
2. Join blocks in each row.
3. Join rows.

Borders

1. Measure length of quilt through middle of quilt top. Trim 2 border strips to match quilt length. Stitch borders to quilt sides, easing to fit as needed.
2. Measure width of quilt through middle of quilt. Trim 2 border strips to match quilt width. Sew borders to top and bottom edges of quilt, easing to fit as needed.

3. Sew black D triangles to adjacent sides of each 1½" C (Diagram B). Press seam allowances toward Ds. Piece 66 C/D units as shown.

4. For top border, join 14 Bs and 15 C/D units in a row (Diagram C). Sew border to top edge of quilt (Quilt Assembly Diagram). Make bottom border in same manner.

5. Join 17 Bs and 18 C/D units in a row to make each side border. Sew borders to quilt sides. Miter border corners.

6. Repeat steps 1 and 2 to add outer black borders.

Quilting and Finishing

1. Mark quilt top with desired quilting design. Quilt shown is machine-quilted in-the-ditch with a floral motif quilted in star centers and a wave pattern in black borders.

2. Layer backing, batting, and quilt top. Baste. Quilt as desired.

3. Make 6⅜ yards of continuous bias or straight-grain binding. Bind quilt edges.

Quilt Assembly Diagram

BOW TIE MEDALLION

Quilt pieced by Jane Strickland of Tamaroa, Illinois;
quilted by Dorothy Yakabovich, Felecita Kellerman, Carol Przygoda, Rigina Heisner, Barb Forys, Carol Porter, Mary Ann Bathon, and Irene Bathon

Combine two sizes of Bow Tie blocks to make this striking king-sized quilt. The diagonal-corners technique makes the blocks quick and easy to stitch.

Finished Size
Quilt: 99" x 99"
Blocks: 140 (6" x 6") Block 1
        56 (6" x 6") Block 2

Materials
35 (9" x 15") scraps bright prints
28 (7" x 9") scraps bright prints
6 yards tan print
1⅝ yards black (includes binding)
3 yards 90"-wide backing fabric

continued

Cutting

Instructions are for rotary cutting and quick piecing. Cut strips cross-grain except as noted. Cut pieces in order listed to get best use of yardage.

From each 9" x 15" scrap

• 8 (3½") A squares.
• 8 (1¾") B squares.

From each 7" x 9" scrap

• 8 (2") C squares.
• 8 (1⅛") D squares.

From tan print

• 10 (6½"-wide) strips for pieced borders or 4 (6½" x 105") length-wise strips. (If cutting lengthwise borders, use leftover to cut A squares.)
• 33 (3½"-wide) strips. From these, cut 392 (3½") A squares.
• 11 (2"-wide) strips. From these, cut 224 (2") C squares.

From black

• 1 yard for binding.
• 8 (2"-wide) strips for borders.

Block Assembly

1. See page 11 for instructions on diagonal-corners quick-piecing technique. Following those instructions, match a B square to 1 corner of a tan A square, right sides facing (Diagram A). Stitch diagonally from corner to corner of B square. Trim excess fabric ¼" from seam. Make 2 A/B units, using matching fabrics.

2. Join 2 A/B units and 2 matching print A squares to complete Bow Tie Block 1 (Block 1 Assembly Diagram). Make 140 of Block 1.

3. Use diagonal-corners method to sew each print D square to a corner of a tan C square.

4. Matching print fabrics, join 2 C/D units and 2 C squares to make a small Bow Tie block. Make 112 small blocks.

5. Join 2 C/D units and 2 tan A squares to complete 1 of Block 2 (Block 2 Assembly Diagram). Make 56 of Block 2.

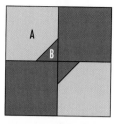

Block 1—Make 140.

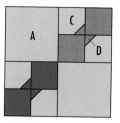

Block 2—Make 56.

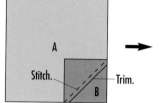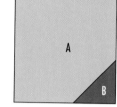

Diagram A

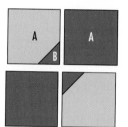

Block 1 Assembly Diagram

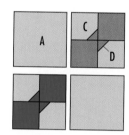

Block 2 Assembly Diagram

Partial Quilt Assembly Diagram

Quilt Assembly

1. Join blocks in quarter sections. Start by laying out 7 of Block 1 in a horizontal row, turning blocks as shown (Partial Quilt Assembly Diagram). For remaining 6 rows, alternate Block 1 and Block 2 as shown in each row.
2. When satisfied with block placement, join blocks in each row. Then join rows.
3. Make 4 quarter-sections.
4. Referring to photo, join 2 sections for top half of quilt and 2 sections for bottom half, rotating sections as shown. Join halves to complete center quilt top.

Borders

1. Join 2 black strips end-to-end to make a border for each quilt side.
2. Measure length of quilt through middle of quilt top. Trim 2 black borders to this measurement. Sew border strips to quilt sides, easing to fit as necessary. Press seam allowances toward borders.
3. Measure width of quilt through the middle and trim remaining black borders to this measurement. Sew borders to top and bottom edges of quilt.
4. Repeat steps 2 and 3 to join tan border strips to each side of quilt.

Quilting and Finishing

1. Mark quilt top with desired quilting design. Quilt shown is outline-quilted and has diagonal lines quilted in borders.
2. Layer backing, batting, and quilt top. Baste. Quilt as desired.
3. Make 11¼ yards of continuous bias or straight-grain binding. Bind quilt edges.

POSTAGE STAMP

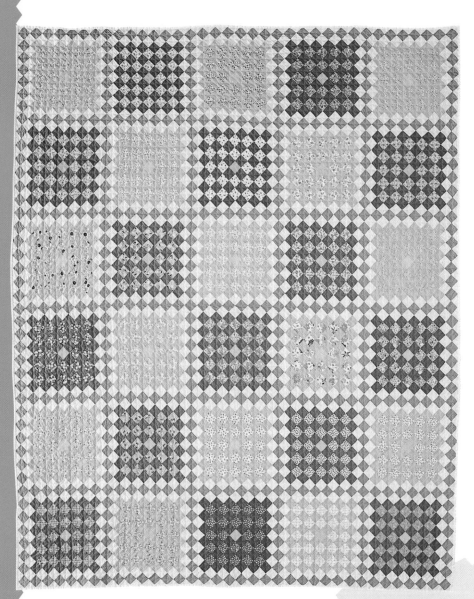

Vintage quilt from the Oxmoor House collection; quiltmaker unknown

Postage Stamp quilts were all the rage during the Depression, when thrifty homemakers put every scrap to good use—even pieces no bigger than a postage stamp. The pretty pastels of this vintage quilt are typical of that period. Let this quilt inspire you to use today's exciting reproduction fabrics to create a quilt that looks complicated but is really easy to sew with our rotary cutting and quick piecing instructions.

Finished Size
Quilt: 76½" x 91½"
Blocks: 50 (10½" x 10½")

Materials
3 yards white
1¾ yards blue solid
1¾ yards pink solid
1½ yards green solid
⅛ yard yellow solid
⅛ yard *each* 15 blue prints
⅛ yard *each* 15 pink prints
⅞ yard binding fabric
5½ yards backing fabric

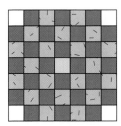

Block 1—Make 15.

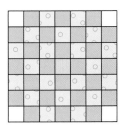

Block 2—Make 15.

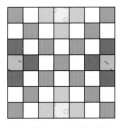

Block 3—Make 20.

Cutting

Instructions are for rotary cutting and quick piecing. Cut all strips cross-grain. Cut pieces in order listed to get best use of yardage.

From white
• 32 (2"-wide) strips for strip sets.
• 4 (3⅜"-wide) strips. From these, cut 39 (3⅜") squares. Cut squares in half diagonally to get 154 edge triangles.
• 2 (2⅜"-wide) squares. Cut squares in half diagonally to get 4 corner triangles.

From blue solid
• 29 (2"-wide) strips for strip sets.

From pink solid
• 29 (2"-wide) strips for strip sets.

From green solid
• 23 (2"-wide) strips. From 4 strips, cut 86 (2") squares for Block 3 and edge blocks.

From yellow solid
• 30 (2") squares for block centers.

From each print fabric
• 2 (2"-wide) strips for strip sets.

Blocks 1 and 2

1. From 1 blue print strip, cut 2 (8") lengths. Cut a matching length of blue solid. Join strips as shown to make 1 of Strip Set A (Strip Set A Diagram). Press seam allowances toward solid fabric. Cut strip set into 4 (2"-wide) segments.

2. From same blue solid strip, cut 2 (16") lengths. Cut a matching length of same blue print used for Strip Set A. Join strips as shown to make 1 of Strip Set B (Strip Set B Diagram). Press seam allowances toward solid fabric. Cut strip set into 8 (2"-wide) segments.

3. Cut a 16" length from each of white, solid blue, and same blue print strips. Join strips to make 1 of Strip Set C (Strip Set C Diagram). Press seam allowances toward blue solid. Cut 8 (2"-wide) segments from strip set as shown.

4. Join 1 each of segments A, B, and C to make a nine-patch (Diagram A). Make 4 nine-patch units.

5. Lay out nine-patches with white square in each outer corner (Block 1 Assembly Diagram). Add yellow square and remaining 4 B units. Join units in 3 horizontal rows. Join rows to complete Block 1.

6. Repeat steps 1–5 to make 15 of Block 1. Pin 4 extra C units to each block as it is completed.

7. Make 15 of Block 2 in same manner, using pink and pink print strips.

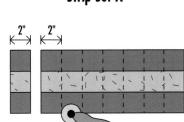

Strip Set A

Strip Set B

Strip Set C

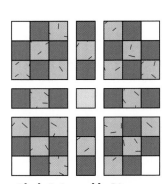

Diagram A

Block 1 Assembly Diagram

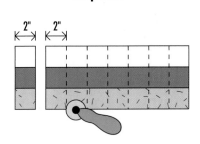

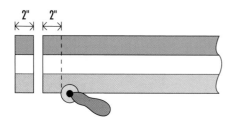

Strip Set D—Make 6.

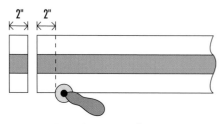

Strip Set E—Make 5.

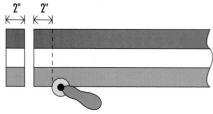

Strip Set F—Make 6.

8. Lay out blocks in diagonal rows as shown (Quilt Assembly Diagram), alternating blue and pink blocks. Each block should have extra C units, which will be used to make adjacent Block 3s.

Block 3

1. Make 5 each of strip sets D, E, and F as shown (Strip Set Diagrams). In each strip set, press seam allowances away from white.
2. Cut 98 (2"-wide) segments from each strip set.
3. Join 1 each of segments D, E, and F to make a nine-patch (Diagram B). Make 98 nine-patches. Set aside 18 for edge blocks.

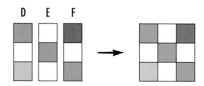

Diagram B

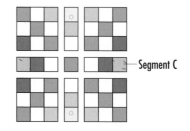

— Segment C

Block 3 Assembly Diagram

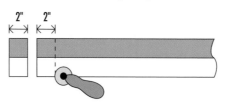

Strip Set G—Make 2.

4. Assemble 1 block at a time, adding each block to quilt layout as it is completed. For first block, lay out 4 nine-patches and 1 green square (Block 3 Assembly Diagram). Between these, place C segments (2 blue, 2 pink) from adjacent blocks. Join units in 3 rows; then join rows to complete Block 3.
5. Make 20 of Block 3.

Edge Blocks

1. Make 1 more of Strip Set D and 1 more of Strip Set F. Press seam allowances away from white. Cut 22 (2"-wide) segments of each strip set.
2. Make 2 of Strip Set G (Strip Set G Diagram). Press seam allowances toward green. Cut these into 44 (2"-wide) segments.

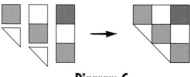

Diagram C

3. For blue units, select 1 each of segments G and F, 1 green square, and 2 white triangles. Sew triangles to green squares (Diagram C); press seam allowances toward green. Join rows to complete unit. Make 22 blue units; then use D segments to make 22 pink units in same manner. Set aside 4 of each color for corner blocks.
4. Join white triangles to 1 side of each remaining green square (Diagram D); press seam allowances toward green. Set aside 4 units for corner blocks.

Diagram D

5. Assemble 1 block at a time, adding each block to quilt layout as it is completed. For first block, lay out 1 each of pink and blue edge units, pink/blue nine-patch, green/white triangle unit, and white edge triangle (Edge Block Assembly Diagram). Add C segments from adjacent blocks as shown. Join segments in rows; then join rows to complete edge block.
6. Make 9 edge blocks as shown, adding each to quilt layout in appropriate position. Then make 9 more blocks, reversing positions of pink and blue.

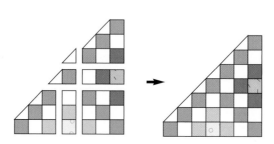

Edge Block Assembly Diagram

Quilt Assembly Diagram

Corner Blocks

1. Join white triangles to opposite sides of each remaining green/white triangle unit; then join corner triangle to top (Diagram E). Make 4 units.

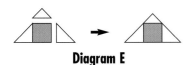

Diagram E

2. Assemble 1 corner at a time. For each corner, lay out 2 matching edge units and 1 corner unit (Corner Block Assembly Diagram). Add C segment from adjacent block as shown. Join units to complete corner block. Make 2 blue corners and 2 pink corners.

Quilt Assembly

1. Join blocks in diagonal rows as shown (Quilt Assembly Diagram).
2. Add a white triangle to each row end.
3. Join rows, matching seam lines carefully.

Quilting and Finishing

1. Mark quilting design on quilt top as desired. Quilt shown has straight lines of quilting that make an X through each square.
2. Layer backing, batting, and quilt top. Baste. Quilt as desired.
3. Make 10 yards of continuous bias or straight-grain binding. Bind quilt edges.

Corner Block Assembly Diagram

OLD THYME CHAIN & STAR

Quilt by Darlene K. Orton of Salina, Kansas

D arlene Orton says she fell in love with this quilt the minute she saw it in *New Jersey Quilts,* published in 1992 by the Heritage Quilt Project of New Jersey, which documented New Jersey's quilt history. Darlene wanted to make her own version of the 1840s-era quilt, staying true to the colors and fabrics of the period. "The patterns were easy," says Darlene. "The challenge was finding enough of the right fabrics." Of course, that's also the *fun* part.

Finished Size
Quilt: 106½" x 121½"
Blocks: 195 (7½" x 7½")

Materials
49 (6" x 22") strips for stars*
188 (2" x 22") strips assorted fabrics (red, pink, brown, blue)*
½ yard red for stars and bows
1½ yards red print for swags
7¾ yards muslin
1 yard binding fabric
9½ yards backing fabric
*Note: 25 (18" x 22") fat quarters are sufficient to cut all strips.

Cutting

Instructions are for rotary cutting. Cut all strips cross-grain except as noted. Cut pieces in order listed to get best use of yardage.

From each star fabric

- 6 (3¼") squares. Cut each square in quarters diagonally to get 24 B triangles, 12 for each of 2 blocks.
- 10 (2") squares. Set aside 2 squares for star centers (A) and 8 squares for block corners (D) for 2 blocks.

From assorted fabric strips

- 97 sets of 4 matched 2" D squares.
- 97 sets of 8 matched 2" E squares.
- 97 sets of 4 matched 2" F squares.
- 97 sets of 4 matched 2" G squares.
- 97 assorted 2" H squares.

To keep track of which sets are which, we recommend putting cut sets in labeled zip-top plastic bags. This way, when you need 4 Ds, for example, you can just reach in and find any 4 squares that match.

From red

- 36 stars.
- 4 bows (4 each X, Y).

From red print

- 22 of side swags.
- 18 top/bottom swags.

From muslin

- 73 (2"-wide) strips. From these, cut 1,533 (2") C squares.
- 4 (5" x 126") lengthwise border strips. Remaining fabric should be approximately 23" wide. Make next 2 cuts from this length.
- 14 (3¼"-wide) strips. From these, cut 98 (3¼") squares. Cut each square in quarters diagonally to get 392 B triangles for star points.
- 39 (2"-wide) strips. From these, cut another 423 (2") C squares to get a total of 1,956 squares.

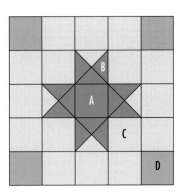

Block 1—Make 98.

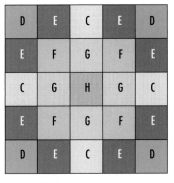

Block 2—Make 97.

Block 1 Assembly

1. For 1 block, choose 1 A square and 12 B triangles of same fabric, 4 muslin B triangles, 16 muslin C squares, and 4 print D squares.
2. Join 1 muslin B and 1 print B (Diagram A). Press seam allowances toward print fabric. Join 2 print Bs as shown. Join pairs to complete 1 star point unit. Make 4 units for each block.

Diagram A

3. Lay out squares and star point units in 5 rows (Block 1 Assembly Diagram). Join squares in each row; then join rows to complete block. Press all row seam allowances in same direction.
4. Make 98 of Block 1.

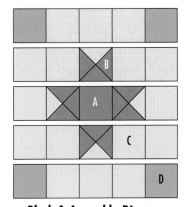

Block 1 Assembly Diagram

Block 2 Assembly

1. For each block, choose 4 muslin C squares and 1 set each of D, E, F, G, and H squares. Lay out squares in 5 rows (Block 2 Assembly Diagram).
2. Join squares in each row.
3. Join rows to complete block. Press all row seam allowances in same direction.
4. Make 97 of Block 2.

continued

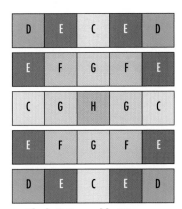

Block 2 Assembly Diagram

Row 1—Make 8.

Row 2—Make 7.

Row Assembly Diagram

Quilt Assembly

1. Lay out blocks in 15 horizontal rows, with 13 blocks in each row. For Row 1 and all odd-numbered rows, start with a star block and alternate blocks as shown (Row Assembly Diagram). For Row 2 and all even-numbered rows, start with Block 2. Turn adjacent blocks as needed to offset seam allowances.
2. Join blocks in each row. Then join rows.
3. Sew 1 border strip to each side of quilt, centering each strip. Miter corners.
4. Referring to photo, pin 9 swags and 8 stars each on top and bottom borders. Pin 11 swags and 10 stars on each side border and bows at border corners at mitered seam. When satisfied with placement, appliqué.

Quilting and Finishing

1. Mark quilt top with desired quilting design. Quilt shown is quilted in-the-ditch around each star, around muslin surrounding each star, and diagonally through each chain square. Echo-quilting surrounds each swag to fill border.
2. Layer backing, batting, and quilt top. Baste. Quilt as desired.
3. Make 13 yards of continuous bias or straight-grain binding. Bind quilt edges.

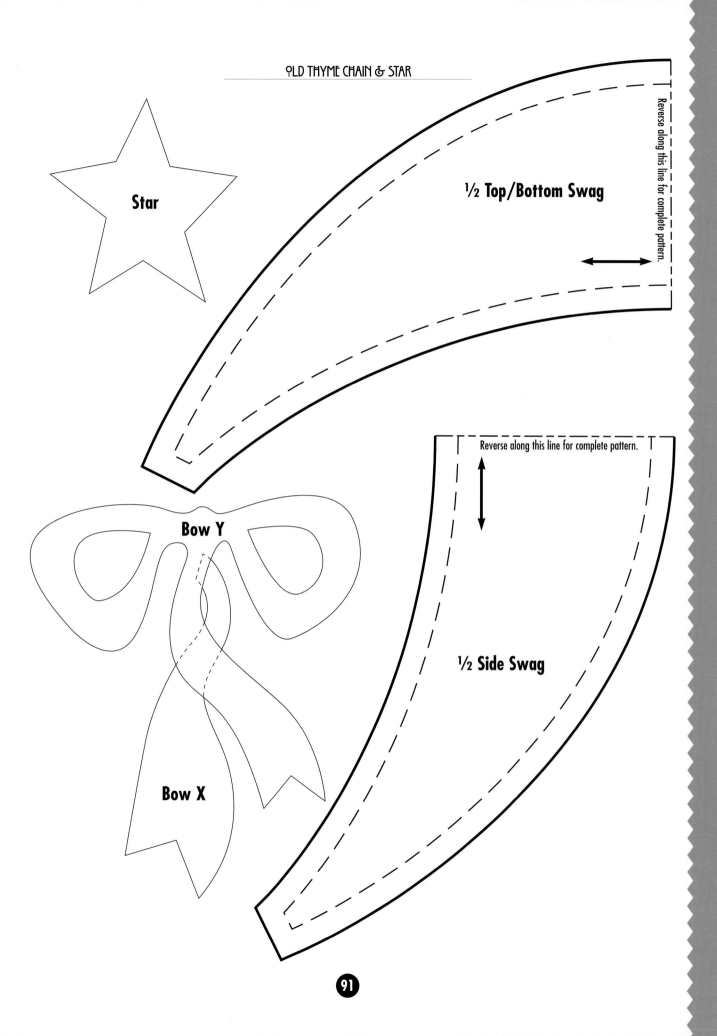

Star

½ Top/Bottom Swag

Reverse along this line for complete pattern.

Reverse along this line for complete pattern.

Bow Y

½ Side Swag

Bow X

PETRONELLA'S GARDEN

Quilt by Ruth R. Easley of Atlanta, Georgia

Ruth Easley created this quilt to showcase 10 blocks she won in her guild's block exchange, plus additional blocks that she made. In a block exchange, each person makes a block in a set color scheme; then one participant wins all the blocks in a drawing.

Finished Size
Quilt: 70" x 82"
Blocks: 12 (10" x 10") flowers
       10 (9¼" x 10") flowers
       1 (20" x 20") center

Materials
30 (6" x 10") scraps for flowers
22 (7") squares assorted green
   scraps for stems and leaves
1 (10") square dark green
½ yard yellow
4 yards white or muslin
2¾ yards green (includes binding)
4½ yards backing fabric

Cutting

Cut all strips cross-grain except as noted. Cut pieces in order listed to get best use of yardage.

From each flower print
- 1 of Pattern B for center block.
- 7 or 8 of Pattern E to get a total of 220 flower petals.

From each 7" green square
- 1 (1" x 8½") bias strip for flower stem.
- 2 of Pattern D.

From dark green
- 3 (1¼" x 12") bias strips for center block flower stems.
- 6 of Pattern A for center block.

From yellow
- 3 of Pattern C for center block.
- 22 of Pattern F for flower blocks.

From white
- 4 (7½"-wide) center border strips.
- 2 (22") squares. Cut squares in half diagonally to get 4 corner triangles.
- 1 (20½") square for center block.
- 6 (10½"-wide) strips. From these, cut 12 (10½") squares and 10 (9¾" x 10½") pieces for flower blocks.

From green
- 1 (10½"-wide) strip. From this, cut 4 (2½" x 10½") X strips and 14 (2⅜" x 10½") sashing strips.
- 4 (2½" x 72") lengthwise strips. From these, cut 4 (2½" x 44") medallion border strips and 4 (2½" x 26") strips for center block.
- 2 (2½" x 47") lengthwise strips for inner borders.
- 6 (2½" x 84") lengthwise strips for outer borders and inner borders.
- 4 (2½" x 84") lengthwise strips for straight-grain binding.

Center Block—Make 1.

Block Assembly

1. Fold 20½" white square in quarters diagonally. Finger-press creases to make appliqué placement guidelines.
2. On each 12" bias strip, fold ¼" to wrong side at 1 end; then fold in ¼" on each long edge. Press.
3. Select 10 B petals for each center flower. Join straight edges of petals to make 1 flower circle.
4. Appliqué 1 C at center of each flower, covering B raw edges.
5. Pin 3 flowers, stems, and 6 A leaves on white square (Center Block Diagram). Tuck unfinished edge of each stem under its flower. When satisfied with placement, appliqué pieces in place.
6. Join 10 E petals in a circle for each flower block. Appliqué 1 F over center of each flower. Make 22 flowers.

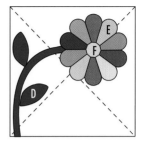

Flower Block—Make 12 (10½" x 10½") blocks and 10 (9¾" x 10½") blocks.

7. Fold each 10½" white square in quarters diagonally; finger-press. Prepare an 8½" bias stem as before and pin stem, 2 D leaves, and flower in place (Flower Block Diagram). When satisfied with placement, appliqué pieces in place. Make 12 (10½") Flower Blocks.
8. Make 10 (9¾" x 10½") flower blocks in same manner, designating 1 (10½") edge of each piece as top of block.

Quilt Assembly

1. Fold 26"-long and 44"-long green strips in half to find centers. Repeat for 7½"-wide white strips. Matching centers, sew long and short green strips to opposite edges of each white strip.
2. Center a combined strip on each edge of center block. Sew strips to block and miter corners.
3. Trim corners of center unit as shown (Trimming Diagram). Discard cut portions. *continued*

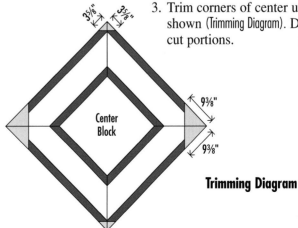

Trimming Diagram

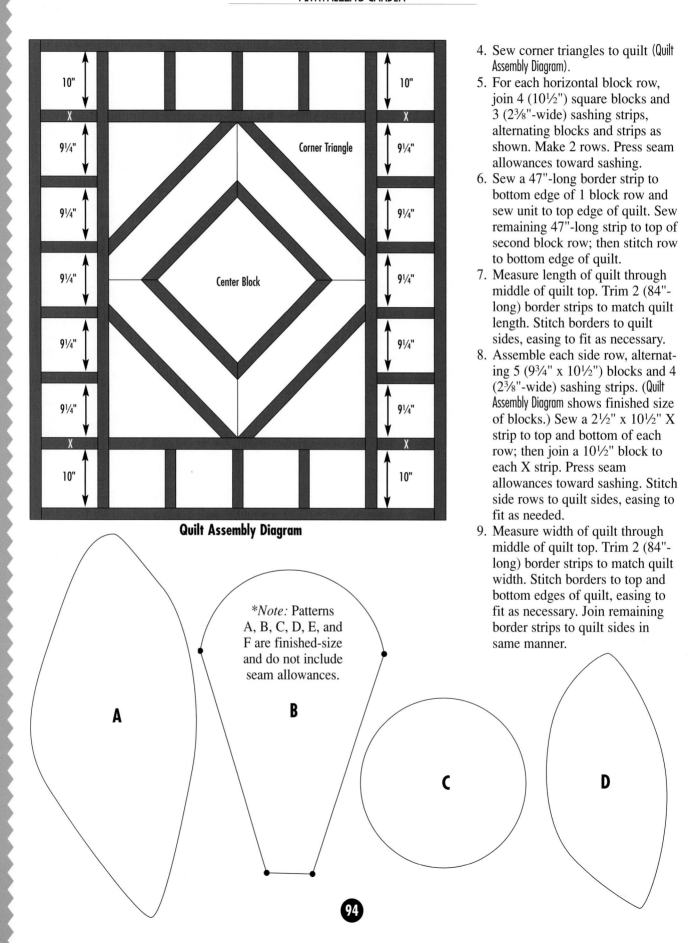

Quilt Assembly Diagram

Note: Patterns A, B, C, D, E, and F are finished-size and do not include seam allowances.

4. Sew corner triangles to quilt (Quilt Assembly Diagram).
5. For each horizontal block row, join 4 (10½") square blocks and 3 (2⅜"-wide) sashing strips, alternating blocks and strips as shown. Make 2 rows. Press seam allowances toward sashing.
6. Sew a 47"-long border strip to bottom edge of 1 block row and sew unit to top edge of quilt. Sew remaining 47"-long strip to top of second block row; then stitch row to bottom edge of quilt.
7. Measure length of quilt through middle of quilt top. Trim 2 (84"-long) border strips to match quilt length. Stitch borders to quilt sides, easing to fit as necessary.
8. Assemble each side row, alternating 5 (9¾" x 10½") blocks and 4 (2⅜"-wide) sashing strips. (Quilt Assembly Diagram shows finished size of blocks.) Sew a 2½" x 10½" X strip to top and bottom of each row; then join a 10½" block to each X strip. Press seam allowances toward sashing. Stitch side rows to quilt sides, easing to fit as needed.
9. Measure width of quilt through middle of quilt top. Trim 2 (84"-long) border strips to match quilt width. Stitch borders to top and bottom edges of quilt, easing to fit as necessary. Join remaining border strips to quilt sides in same manner.

Quilting and Finishing

1. Mark quilt top with desired quilting design. Quilt shown has outline quilting around flower petals, leaves, stems, and block seams, plus stipple quilting in background of center block. Patterns for medallion border design, corner feather wreath, and bow are on page 96. Cross-hatching in border is 1½"-wide and ¾"-wide in corner triangles.

2. Layer backing, batting, and quilt top. Baste. Quilt as desired.

3. From remaining green strips, make 8⅝ yards of straight-grain binding. Bind quilt edges.

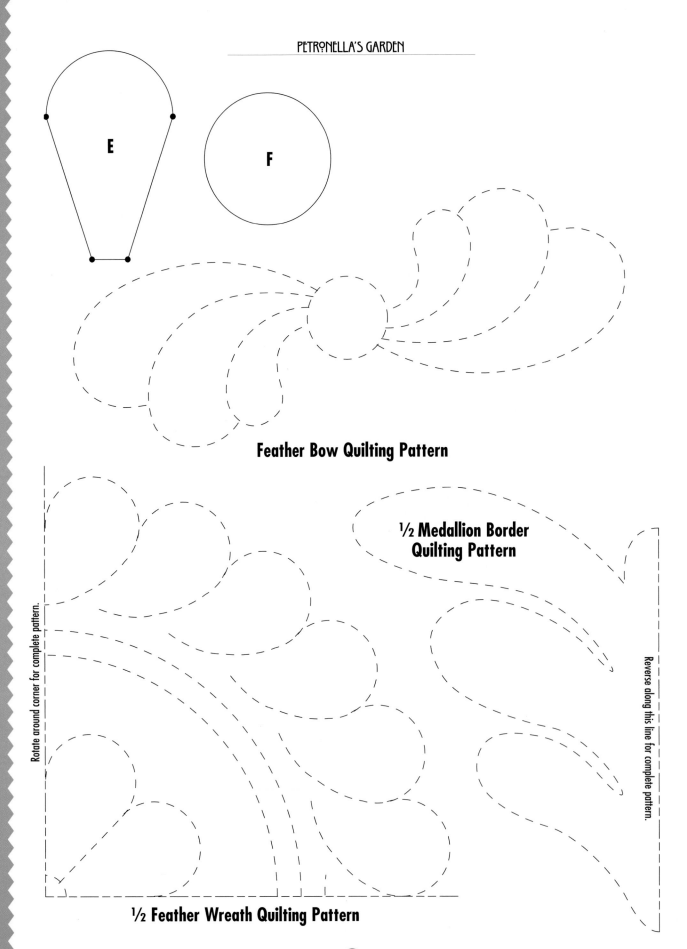

E

F

Feather Bow Quilting Pattern

½ Medallion Border Quilting Pattern

Rotate around corner for complete pattern.

Reverse along this line for complete pattern.

½ Feather Wreath Quilting Pattern

PINE BURR

Marion Watchinski loves neatly matched seams and sharply sewn points, but found these intimidating until she discovered foundation piecing. She used dark fabrics to capture the look of a nineteenth-century quilt, but you can create your own color scheme—pretty pastels or rainbow brights will work just as well. Our instructions show you how to quick-piece this classic quilt block.

Finished Size
Quilt: 86" x 98"
Blocks: 42 (12" x 12")

Materials
42 (9" x 22") fat eighths light prints for blocks
42 (18" x 22") fat quarters dark prints for blocks
7½ yards dark green print (includes binding)
2⅝ yards 90"-wide backing fabric
continued

Quilt by Marion Roach Watchinski of Overland Park, Kansas

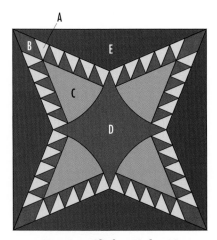

Pine Burr Block—Make 42.

Cutting

Instructions are for rotary cutting and quick piecing, except as noted. Make templates for patterns B, C, D, and E on pages 100 and 101. Patterns A and F are provided if you prefer traditional piecing. Cut all strips cross-grain except as noted. Cut pieces in order listed to get best use of yardage.

From each *light print*

- 3 (1⅞" x 22") strips for quick-pieced A units.
- 4 (1⅞") squares. Cut squares in half diagonally to get 8 A triangles.

From each *dark print*

- 3 (1⅞" x 22") strips for quick-pieced A units.
- 4 of Pattern B.
- 1 of Pattern D.
- 4 of Pattern C.

From remaining dark prints

- 26 (3⅞" x 7¾") rectangles for border triangle-squares (F).

From dark green print

- Set aside ⅞ yard for binding.
- 12 (13"-wide) strips. From these, cut 168 of Pattern E, placing straight edge of pattern on 13" length.
- 6 (3⅞"-wide) strips. From these, cut 26 (3⅞" x 7¾") pieces for border triangle-squares (F).
- 16 (2½"-wide) strips for borders.
- 1 (7½"-wide) strip. From this, cut 4 (7½") border squares.

Block Assembly

Note: Each block has 32 A triangle-squares, 8 additional light A triangles, 4 B diamonds, 4 Cs, 1 D, and 4 Es (Block Diagram). All pieces in a group (i.e., 4 Cs) are same fabric. In most blocks, dark As, Bs, and D match.

1. Choose 1 light 1⅞"-wide strip for triangle-squares. On wrong side of strip, mark 16 (1⅞") squares (Diagram A). Draw a diagonal line through each square as shown.

2. Match light strip with a dark strip, right sides facing. Stitch a ¼" seam on *both* sides of each diagonal line. Cut units apart on all drawn lines to get 32 A triangle-square units. Press seam allowances toward dark fabric.

3. Join 4 A units in a row. Add 1 A triangle to end of row (Diagram B). Sew row to side of 1 C.

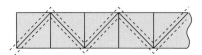

Diagram A

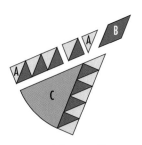

Diagram B

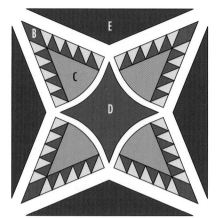

Block Assembly Diagram

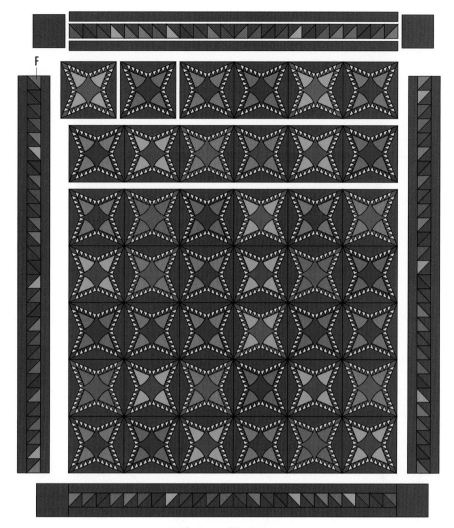

Quilt Assembly Diagram

4. Make another row of A units, orienting triangles as shown. Add B to end of row; then sew row to opposite side of C. Make 4 matching quadrants for each block.
5. Stitch quadrants to curved edges of piece D (Block Assembly Diagram).
6. Add 4 Es to complete block. Make 42 Pine Burr blocks.

Quilt Assembly

1. Lay out blocks in 7 horizontal rows with 6 blocks in each row (Quilt Assembly Diagram). Arrange blocks to get a pleasing balance of color and value. When satisfied with block placement, join blocks in each row.
2. Join rows.

Borders

1. On wrong side of each green 3⅞" x 7¾" rectangle, mark 2 (3⅞") squares. Draw a diagonal line through each square as before.
2. Match each green rectangle with a dark print rectangle, right sides facing. Stitch, cut, and press as before to make 104 F triangle-square units.
3. Join 2 (2½"-wide) green strips end-to-end to make 8 border strips.
4. Measure length of quilt through middle of quilt top. Trim 4 strips to match quilt length for side borders. Measure width of quilt

through middle and trim remaining 4 strips to match width.
5. Join 28 F triangle-squares in a row for each side border, changing direction of triangles mid-row as shown (Quilt Assembly Diagram). Sew trimmed border strips to both sides of F rows, easing to fit as needed. Press seam allowances toward border strips.
6. Stitch side borders to quilt sides, easing to fit.
7. For top and bottom borders, join 24 F triangle-squares in a row, changing direction of triangles mid-row as shown. Sew remaining border strips to both sides of 24-unit F rows, easing to fit as

needed. Press seam allowances toward border strips.
8. Add a 7½" green square to each end of top and bottom borders. Stitch borders to top and bottom edges of quilt.

Quilting and Finishing

1. Mark quilt top with desired quilting design. Quilt shown is quilted with concentric circles centered on each block intersection.
2. Layer backing, batting, and quilt top. Baste. Quilt as desired.
3. Make 10½ yards of continuous straight-grain or bias binding. Bind quilt edges.

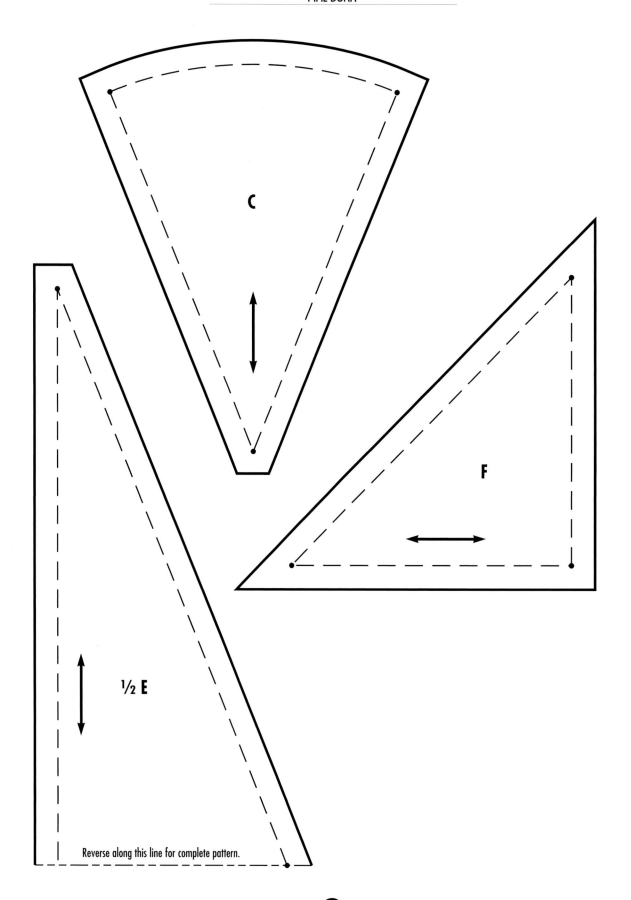

C

F

½ E

Reverse along this line for complete pattern.

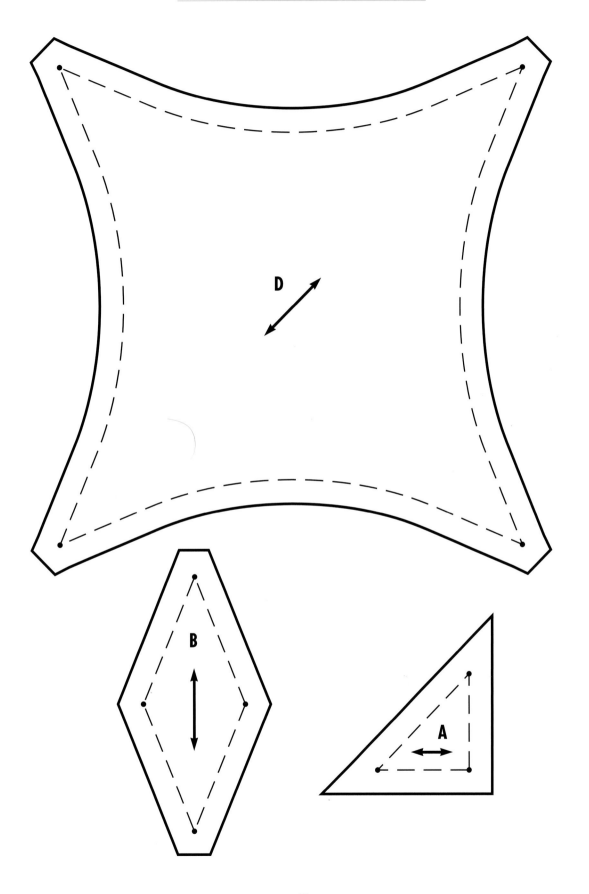

D

B

A

CHARADE

Quilt by Lou Beasley of Centralia, Missouri

The inner border in this quilt gave Lou Beasley a chance to show off her quilting skills as well as her design savvy. She used reproduction fabrics to capture the look of quilts she grew up with.

Finished Size

Quilt: 82½" x 94½"
Blocks: 184 (4½" x 4½")

Materials

12 (18" x 22") fat quarters prints
6 (⅝-yard) pieces pastel solids
4 yards white or muslin
4⅝ yards green (includes binding)
2⅞ yards 90"-wide backing fabric

Cutting

Instructions combine rotary cutting, strip piecing, and traditional piecing. Make templates for patterns B, C, and D on page 104. Use Pattern A for nine-patch square only if you prefer traditional piecing rather than strip piecing. Cut strips cross-grain except as noted. Cut pieces in order listed to get best use of yardage.
From each *print fat quarter*
• 8 (2" x 22") strips for strip piecing.
From each *pastel solid*
• 8 (2¼"-wide) strips. From these, cut 492 of Pattern B (123 groups of 4).
From white
• 6 (3"-wide) strips. From these, cut 104 of Pattern D.
• 4 (5" x 72") border strips.
• 84 (2" x 22") strips for blocks.
From green
• 1 (34") square for binding.
• 2 (2" x 75") border strips.
• 37 (1¼"-wide) strips. From these and fabric leftover from border cut, cut 596 of Pattern C.

Nine-Patch Block—Make 184.

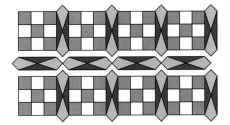

Strip Set 1—Make 36.

Strip Set 2—Make 24.

Block Assembly

1. For Strip Set 1, join 2 matching print strips to both sides of a white strip (Strip Set 1 Diagram). Press all seam allowances in same direction. Make 36 of Strip Set 1.

2. For Strip Set 2, join white strips to both sides of each remaining print strip (Strip Set 2 Diagram). Press all seam allowances in same direction. Make 24 of Strip Set 2.

3. For each block, cut 2 (2"-wide) segments of Strip Set 1 and 1 (2"-wide) segment of Strip Set 2, matching print fabrics. Sew Strip Set 1 segments to both sides of Strip Set 2 segment, turning segments to offset seam allowances.

4. Make 184 nine-patch blocks, 15 of each fabric and 4 extra.

Quilt Assembly

1. Lay out 80 nine-patch blocks in 10 horizontal rows with 8 blocks in each row. Leave room between blocks and between rows for sashing units (Quilt Assembly Diagram).

2. For each sashing unit, join 2 Cs and 2 Bs of different pastel solids (Sashing Unit Diagram). Make 194 sashing units, inserting each unit into quilt layout as it is assembled so you can match colors of adjacent Bs. Set aside 52 sashing units for outer borders.

Sashing Unit— Make 194.

Outer Sashing Unit— Make 104.

3. When satisfied with layout, join blocks and sashing units in each row, leaving B points extending beyond block as shown (Row Assembly Diagram).

4. To add sashing row, stitch sashing units to blocks in previous row, leaving B points extending as before. Then stitch set-in seams to join Bs. Leave B points at top, bottom, and row ends.

continued

Row Assembly Diagram

Quilt Assembly Diagram

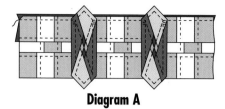

Diagram A

Borders

1. Align raw edges of 1 side of quilt with 1 green border strip, right sides facing, with quilt on top. Stitch from edge of quilt to seam of first B and backstitch. Skip to opposite seam of first B, backstitch to lock seam, and stitch to seam of second B (Diagram A). Continue stitching blocks to border, skipping Bs, to end of border.

2. Press seam allowances toward border. Trim border strip even with top and bottom edges of quilt. On right side of quilt, appliqué B points onto border.

3. Repeat steps 1 and 2 for second side border. Then add top and bottom borders in same manner. Trim top and bottom borders even with edges of side borders.

4. Measure length of quilt through middle of quilt top. Trim 2 white borders to match length. Stitch white borders to quilt sides.

5. Measure width of quilt through middle of quilt top, including side borders. Trim remaining white borders to match quilt width. Stitch borders to top and bottom edges of quilt top.

6. Repeat steps 4 and 5 to add outer green border strips. Press seam allowances toward green borders.

Pieced Border

1. For each side border, lay out 2 vertical rows with 12 blocks in each row. Leave room between blocks for sashing. Between rows, add 12 sashing units, matching colors of adjacent Bs.

2. To make each outer sashing unit, join 2 Cs, 1 B, and 1 D (Outer Sashing Unit Diagram). Make 26 units for each side border, inserting each unit into border layout as it is assembled so you can match colors of adjacent Bs.

3. When satisfied with arrangement of side borders, join blocks and sashing units in each border, setting in seams as before. Stitch completed borders to quilt sides.

4. For top border, lay out 2 rows of 14 blocks, 2 sashing units, and 26 outer sashing units. Between rows, lay out 12 sashing units as before. Join blocks and sashing units; then stitch border to top edge of quilt. Make bottom border in same manner.

Quilting and Finishing

1. Mark quilt top with desired quilting design. On quilt shown, Bs and Ds are outline-quilted and an "X" is quilted through each nine-patch square. Look for a commercial quilting stencil that will fit white border or design your own.

2. Layer backing, batting, and quilt top. Baste. Quilt as desired.

3. Make 10 yards of continuous bias or straight-grain binding. Bind quilt edges.

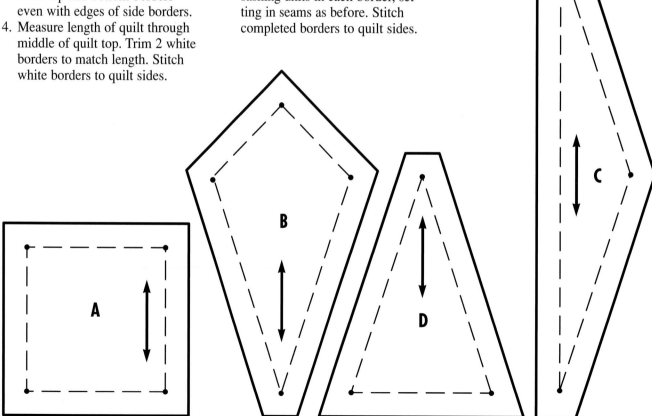

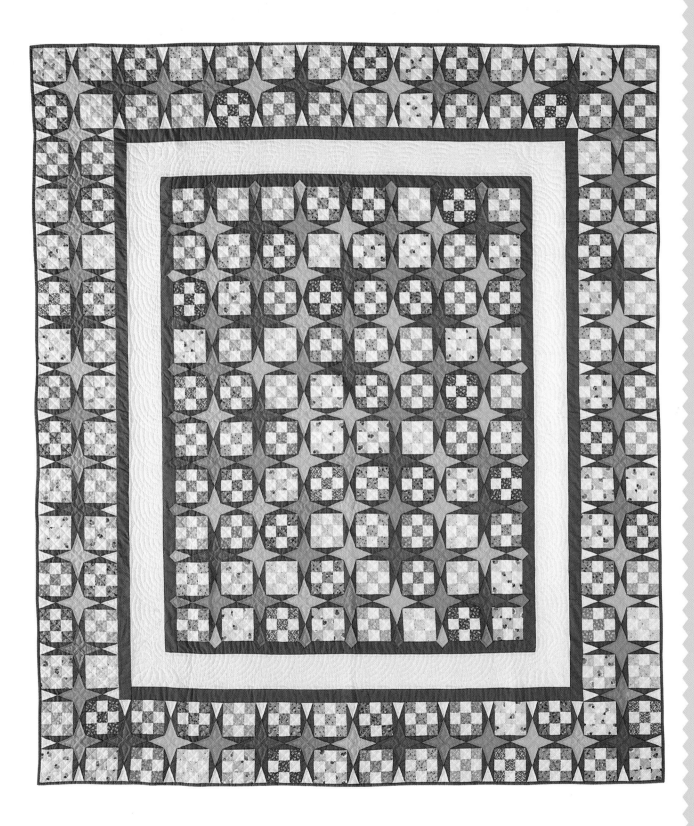

DIZZY GEESE

Quilt by Joan K. Streck of Overland Park, Kansas

"I always come away from a workshop with at least one new idea," says Joan Streck. A class on design and use of the traditional Flying Geese motif gave Joan the idea for Dizzy Geese. "I had an old pattern called Tiled Wedding Ring that I wanted to use in a new way," Joan recalls. She redrew the design with a star inside a ring of flying geese and squared off the block with a corner triangle. This is Joan's first attempt at designing a quilt "from scratch." In addition to designing the block, she added pieced sashing to create small stars between blocks.

Finished Size
Quilt: 74½" x 93"
Blocks: 12 (17" x 17")

Materials
8½ yards cream tone-on-tone print (includes binding)
15 (18" x 22") fat quarters or scraps (mostly solids, plaids, and stripes)
⅛ yard tan print
5⅝ yards backing fabric

Dizzy Geese Block—Make 12.

Cutting

Instructions are for rotary cutting and quick piecing, except as noted. Make templates for patterns C, D, and H on page 108. Cut all strips cross-grain except as noted. Cut pieces in order listed to get best use of yardage.

From cream

- Set aside 2½ yards for borders and binding.
- 13 (2¾"-wide) strips. From these, cut 48 (2¾") B squares and 104 of Pattern H.
- 3 (4"-wide) strips. From these, cut 48 of Pattern D.
- 42 (2"-wide) strips. From these, cut 576 (2") E squares and 176 (2" x 3½") F pieces.
- 3 (4⅛"-wide) strips. From these, cut 26 (4⅛") squares. Cut each square in half diagonally to get 52 G triangles.
- 8 (6"-wide) strips. From these, cut 26 (6") squares. Cut squares in half diagonally to get 52 I triangles.
- 1 (17½"-wide") strip. From this, cut 17 (2" x 17½") sashing strips.
- 24 (1¼") K squares.

From scraps

- 12 (5") A squares.
- 12 same-fabric sets of 4 of Pattern C and 4 of Pattern C reversed (1 set for each block).
- 48 (2" x 21") strips. From these, cut 288 (2" x 3½") F rectangles.
- 32 (2"-wide) strips. From these, cut 352 (2") E squares.

From tan print

- 6 (2") J squares.
- 48 (1¼") K squares.

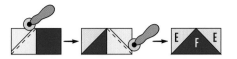

Diagram A

Block Assembly

1. For each block, select 1 A, 4 B squares, 4 Ds, and 1 set of C and C rev. triangles.
2. See instructions on page 11 for diagonal-corner quick-piecing technique. Following those instructions, sew B squares to 4 corners of A square. Press seam allowances toward A.
3. Sew C and C rev. triangles to sides of each D (Block Diagram). Press seam allowances toward D. Make 4 C/D units.
4. Select 24 scrap F rectangles and 48 cream E squares. Use diagonal-corner technique to sew an E to 2 corners of each F to make a Fly-ing Geese unit (Diagram A). Press seam allowances toward Es.
5. Join 3 geese units in a row. Make 8 geese rows.
6. Select 4 rows for corners. Sew H pieces to both ends of each row (Block Assembly Diagram). Press seam allowances toward H. Then sew G and I triangles to opposite sides of unit as shown. Press seam allowances toward G and I. Make 4 corner units.

Diagram B

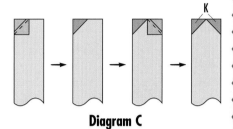

Diagram C

7. Sew remaining 4 geese rows to D edge of C/D units. Press seam allowances toward D.
8. Lay out units in 3 horizontal rows as shown (Block Assembly Diagram). Join units in rows; then join rows to complete block.
9. Make 12 blocks.

Quilt Assembly

1. Using diagonal-corner technique, sew cream K squares to 4 corners of each J square (Diagram B). In same manner, sew tan K squares to 1 end of each sashing strip (Diagram C). Set aside 10 strips; then sew remaining tan squares to opposite end of remaining 7 sashing strips. *continued*

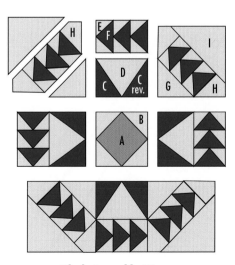

Block Assembly Diagram

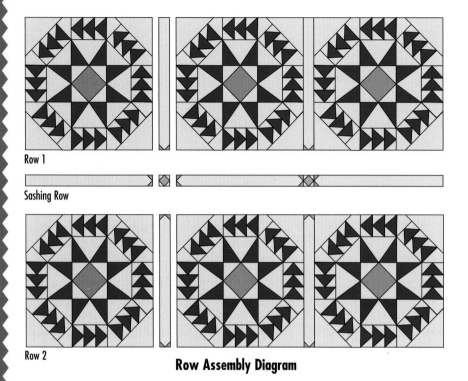

Row 1

Sashing Row

Row 2

Row Assembly Diagram

2. Lay out 2 rows of 3 blocks each, inserting sashing between blocks (Row Assembly Diagram). For Row 1, use sashing with 1 sewn end. For Row 2, use sashing with 2 sewn ends. Between block rows, lay out a Sashing Row as shown. When satisfied with placement, join units in each row. Repeat to make bottom half of quilt.

3. Referring to photo, lay out rows to verify placement. Join rows to complete quilt center.

Borders

1. Use scrap E squares and cream Fs to make 176 Flying Geese units for borders.

2. From fabric reserved for borders, cut 4 (3¾"-wide) lengths for inner border and 4 (4½"-wide) lengths for outer border. Save remainder for binding.

3. Measure quilt length through middle of pieced top. Trim 2 inner

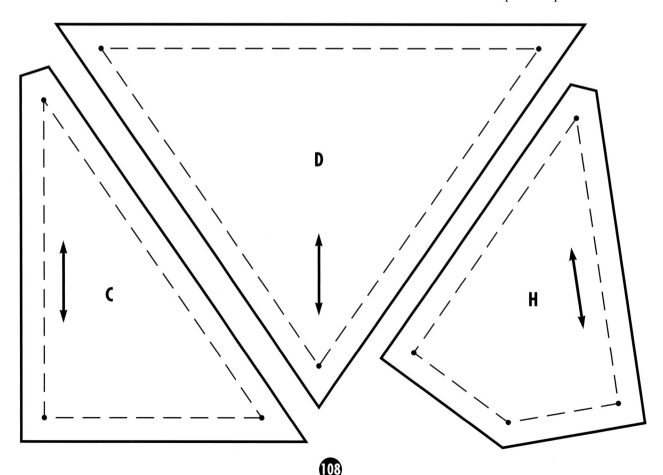

border strips to match length. Measure width of pieced top through middle; trim remaining inner border strips to match width.

4. For each side border, sew 46 geese end-to-end. Match length of geese row with precut side border. You have enough geese units to add 1 more if needed to match border length. Sew geese rows to side borders, referring to photo for correct position of each row. (Note that on left border, geese fly south; on right border, they fly north.) Ease geese to fit borders as needed. Then sew joined borders to quilt sides, easing to fit quilt top. Press all seam allowances toward cream border.

5. Join 34 geese end-to-end for top border. Match length to precut top border, adding 1 more geese unit if needed. Sew geese to top border with geese flying west. Repeat for bottom border, positioning geese flying east.

6. Join 3 geese units with G, H, and I pieces to make each corner unit as before. Referring to photo, sew corners to ends of top and bottom borders.

7. Sew borders to top and bottom edges of quilt top.

8. Measure length of quilt through middle as before. Trim 2 outer border strips to match length. Sew these to quilt sides, easing to fit as needed. Repeat for top and bottom borders. Press seam allowances toward outer borders.

Quilting and Finishing

1. Mark quilt top with desired quilting design. Quilt shown is outline-quilted with a cable quilted in each cream border.

2. Layer backing, batting, and quilt top. Baste. Quilt as desired.

3. Make 9½ yards of continuous straight-grain binding from remaining cream fabric. Bind quilt edges.

STARS OF YESTERDAY

Quilt by Kristi Hammer of Yuma, Arizona

Inspired by an antique quilt, Kristi Hammer used reproduction fabrics to make these pink and brown Union Star blocks. Kristi changed the value placement in each block to make the piecing a challenge. She selected a pink-and-brown print for the border that ties it all together. Our instructions call for equal amounts of pink and brown (ranging from pale pink and barely tan to almost-red and deep chocolate), but you can use as many fabrics as you like, or more of one color than another, if you prefer.

Finished Size
Quilt: 70" x 84"
Blocks: 20 (12" x 12")

Materials
14" x 22" piece *each* 10 pink prints and 10 brown prints (includes binding)
9" x 16" piece *each* 20 light shirting prints for block backgrounds
1¾ yards light tan for sashing
2⅛ yards border fabric
4¼ yards 45"-wide backing fabric or 2⅛ yards 90"-wide backing

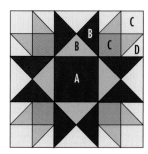

Union Square Block—Make 20.

Cutting

Instructions are for rotary cutting and quick piecing. Cut all strips cross-grain except as noted. For traditional cutting and piecing, use patterns on page 112. Cut pieces in order listed to get best use of yardage.

From each pink and brown print
- 1 (2½" x 22") strip for binding.*
- 1 (8") square for D triangle-squares.
- 3 (5¼") squares. Cut each square in quarters diagonally to get 12 B triangles.
- 1 (4½") A square.
- 4 (2½") C squares.

Note: Pieces are for 20 blocks. Mix and match fabrics as desired.

From each background fabric
- 1 (8") square for D triangle-squares.
- 1 (5¼") square. Cut square in quarters diagonally to get 4 B triangles.
- 4 (2½") C squares.

From sashing fabric
- 6 (2½" x 60") lengthwise strips.
- 13 (2½" x 28") strips. From these, cut 25 (2½" x 12½") sashing strips.

From border fabric
- 4 (6½" x 75") lengthwise strips.*
* Use remaining border fabric for straight-grain binding, if desired.

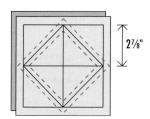

2⅞"

Diagram A

Block Assembly

1. On wrong side of each 8" square of background fabric, mark a 2-square by 2-square grid of 2⅞" squares, leaving a 1" margin on all sides (Diagram A). Draw diagonal lines through squares as shown.
2. Match each marked piece with an 8" square of pink or brown fabric, right sides facing. Stitch ¼" seam on both sides of diagonal lines. (Red line on diagram shows first continuous stitching path; blue line shows second path.) Press. Cut on all drawn lines to get 8 D triangle-squares.
3. For 1 block, select 4 Bs, 4 Cs, and 8 D triangle-squares, all with same background fabric. From pink and brown prints, choose 1 A square, 4 B triangles of 1 print and 8 Bs of another print, and 4 C squares.
4. For each corner unit, join a print C square, a background C square, and 2 D triangle-squares as shown (Diagram B). Make 4 corner units. Press seam allowances toward Cs.
5. For each triangle unit, join B triangles in pairs as shown (Diagram C). Press seam allowances toward same fabric in each pair. Join pairs to complete unit. Make 4 triangle units.
6. Lay out 4 corner units, 4 triangle units, and A square in 3 rows as shown (Block Assembly Diagram). Position triangle units with background fabric at outside edge and corner units with background C square in outside corner.

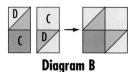

Diagram B

Diagram C

7. Sew triangle units to opposite sides of A square. Sew corner units to remaining triangle units as shown. Press seam allowances toward triangle units.
8. Join rows to complete block.
9. Make 20 blocks, varying fabrics and value placement as desired.

Quilt Assembly

1. Referring to photo, lay out blocks in 5 horizontal rows with 4 blocks in each row. Lay 12½" sashing strips between blocks and at row ends. Move blocks around to get a nice balance of color and value.
2. When satisfied with block placement, join blocks and sashing strips in each row. Press seam allowances toward sashing.
3. Lay out rows again, placing 60" sashing strips between rows. Join rows and sashing, trimming sashing strips to fit.

Border

1. Measure length of quilt through middle of quilt top. Trim 2 border strips to match length. Stitch border strips to quilt sides, easing to fit as needed. Press seam allowances toward borders.
2. Measure width of quilt through middle of quilt top and trim remaining borders to fit. Sew border strips to top and bottom edges of quilt, easing to fit.

continued

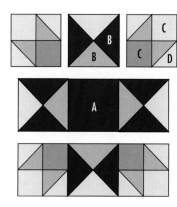

Block Assembly Diagram

Quilting and Finishing

1. Mark quilt top with desired quilting design. On quilt shown, blocks are outline-quilted. Create your own design for sashings and border, or look for commercial stencils to fit those areas.

2. Layer backing, batting, and quilt top. Baste. Quilt as desired.

3. For pieced binding as shown, sew 15 (2½" x 22") strips end-to-end to get 8¾ yards of continuous straight-grain binding. If you prefer, you can make continuous bias or straight-grain binding from a single fabric. Bind quilt edges.

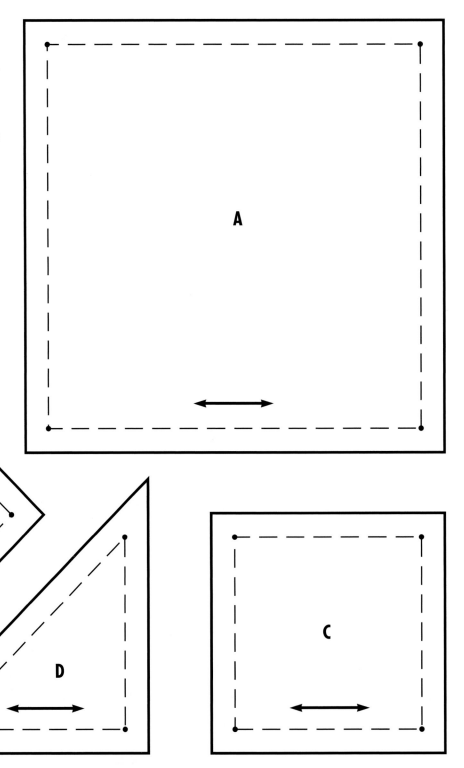

WREATH IN THE WINDOW

"Group quilts are great fun, and a real plus for busy people," says Mary Lou Watson, one of seven women who call themselves Pieceful Scrappers. Even a big quilt like this one required each member to make just eight blocks. The group meets weekly to spend many a productive hour quilting (and chatting) around a large frame.

The Scrappers created the effect of Attic Windows by using two cream tone-on-tone prints, one slightly darker than the other, for the outer pieces of the block. The scrap fabrics coordinate with the border fabric, a floral print that "we chose thinking that corner miters would be easy," according to Mary Lou. "We were wrong, but we did it!"

Quilt by the Pieceful Scrappers of Toronto, Canada

Finished Size

Quilt: 98½" x 108½"*
Blocks: 56 (12" x 12")
*Note: This is a king-size quilt. For a 86½" x 98½" queen-size, make 42 blocks, set 6 across and 7 down.

Materials

3⅜ yards muslin
3¼ yards border fabric (includes binding)
2 yards each of 2 beige/tan tone-on-tone prints
½ yard inner border fabric
166 (5" x 9") scraps
8¾ yards backing fabric

continued

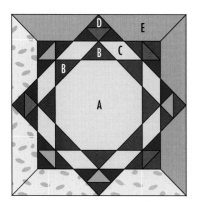

**Wreath in the Window
Block—Make 56.**

Cutting

Make templates for patterns C and E on page 115. All other instructions are for rotary cutting and quick piecing. Cut all strips cross-grain. Cut pieces in order listed to get best use of yardage.

From muslin
- 56 (6½") A squares.
- 28 (1¾"-wide) strips. From these, cut 448 of Pattern C.

From each beige/tan print
- 224 of Pattern E.

From inner border fabric
- 12 (1¼"-wide) strips. Add remaining fabric to scraps.

From scraps
- Set aside 56 scraps for block's inner circle (wreath). From remainder, cut 896 (2⅛") squares. Cut each square in half diagonally to get 1,792 D triangles.

Block Assembly

1. For each block, select 1 A, 8 Cs, 4 Es of each beige/tan fabric, 32 Ds, and 1 (5" x 9") scrap.

2. From scrap, cut a 3¾" square. Cut this in quarters diagonally to get 4 B triangles. From remaining scrap, cut 4 (2¼") squares.

3. See page 11 for instructions on diagonal-corner technique. Sew B squares to 4 corners of A square (Diagram A). Press seam allowances toward A.

4. Sew C diamonds to sides of each B triangle (Diagram B). Press seam allowances toward Cs. Make 4 B/C units.

5. Select 4 D triangles. Join 2 triangles to make a square; then add 2 more triangles to adjacent sides of square as shown (Diagram C). Make 8 D units.

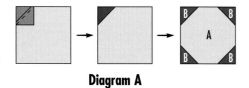

Diagram A

Diagram B

Diagram C

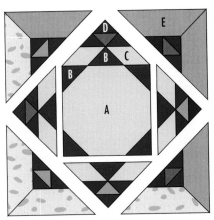

Block Assembly Diagram

6. Sew a D unit to top of each B/C unit (Block Assembly Diagram). Sew 2 joined units to opposite sides of A/B square as shown. Press. Sew 2 units to remaining sides of A/B.

7. To make corner units, sew 2 Es to adjacent sides of each remaining D unit, mitering corners as shown (Corner Unit Diagram). Select Es carefully, referring to block diagrams for correct placement of beige/tan fabrics. Press seam allowances toward Es.

8. Sew corner units to block as shown to complete block. Make 56 blocks.

Corner Unit

Quilt Assembly

1. Referring to photo, lay out blocks in 8 horizontal rows of 7 blocks each. All blocks are positioned in same manner, not turned, so adjacent E pieces are always contrasting fabrics.

2. When satisfied with block placement, join blocks in rows.

3. Join rows to complete quilt center.

Borders

1. Cut 4 (6"-wide) lengthwise strips from outer border fabric. Set aside remainder for binding.

2. Join inner border strips end-to-end to get 4 (115"-long) strips. Sew an inner border strip to one edge of each outer border, matching center points.

3. Sew borders to quilt, mitering corners.

Quilting and Finishing

1. Mark quilt top with desired quilting design. Quilt shown is outline-quilted with a floral design quilted in center of each block and a lover's knot quilted in X formed by E pieces where blocks meet.

2. Layer backing, batting, and quilt top. Baste. Quilt as desired.

3. Make 11¾ yards of continuous bias or straight-grain binding. Bind quilt edges.

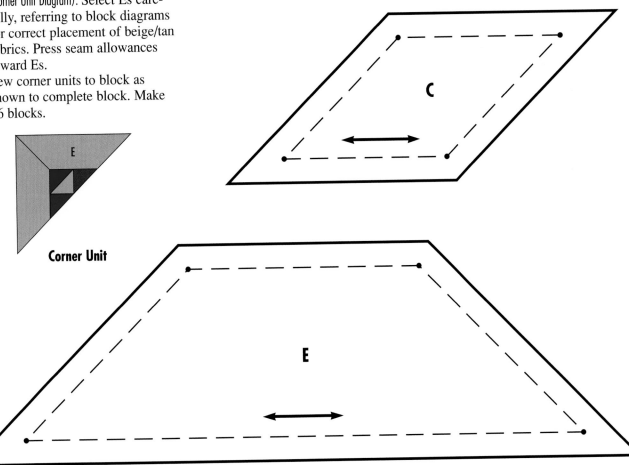

C

E

TULIP GARDEN WEDDING

Quilt by Elsie M. Campbell of Montrose, Pennsylvania

This lovely quilt was born out of a class Elsie Campbell taught on making Double Wedding Ring quilts. She made a small sample for the class, but she liked it so much that she had to make it a full-size quilt. Elsie added appliquéd red tulips at the request of a friend so he could make the quilt an anniversary gift for his wife. Elsie's beautiful trapuntoed quilting makes this quilt a real standout.

Finished Size

Quilt: 84" x 84"
Blocks: 88 (4½" x 10") partial rings

Materials

20 (18" x 22") fat quarters of assorted solids fabrics for arcs
½ yard *each* dark red, medium red, and dark green for appliqué
4½ yards mint (includes binding)
4½ yards white or muslin
2½ yards 90"-wide backing fabric
10 yards ¹⁄₁₆"-diameter soft cording for piping
Stuffing for trapunto (optional)

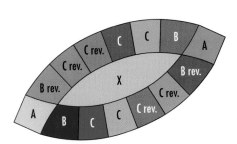

Partial Ring—Make 88.

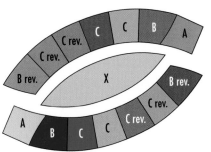

Partial Ring Assembly Diagram

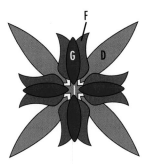

Four-Tulip Diagram

Cutting

Make templates of patterns A, B, C, X, and Y for piecing and patterns D–I for appliqué (pages 120 and 121). Cut pieces in order listed to get best use of yardage.

From each solid fat quarter
- 7 (2½" x 22") strips to get a total of 126 strips. Mixing fabrics together, from these, cut
  - 184 of Pattern A.
  - 176 of Pattern B.
  - 176 of Pattern B reversed.
  - 352 of Pattern C.
  - 352 of Pattern C reversed.

From dark green
- 76 of Pattern D (leaf).
- 4 of Pattern E (partial stem).
- 16 of Pattern H (half stem).
- 5 of Pattern I (complete stem).

From dark red
- 56 of Pattern F.

From medium red
- 56 of Pattern G.

From mint
- 1 yard for binding.
- 4 (6½" x 90") lengthwise strips for outer border.
- 48 of Pattern X.
- 16 of Pattern Y.

From white
- 9 (1"-wide) strips for piping.
- 2 (31¾") squares. Cut squares in half diagonally to get 4 Z triangles.
- 4 (8" x 90") lengthwise strips for appliqué border.
- 40 of Pattern X.
- 9 of Pattern Y.

Partial Ring Assembly

1. For each partial ring, join 1 B reversed, 2 Cs reversed, 2 Cs, 1 B, and 1 A into an arc as shown (Partial Ring Assembly Diagram). For second arc, join A, B, 2 Cs, 2 Cs reversed, and 1 B reversed.

2. Sew both arcs to opposite sides of X piece (Partial Ring Diagram). Stitch seams to join As to B reversed of opposite arc. Press seam allowances away from X.

3. Complete 48 partial rings with green Xs and 40 with white Xs.

Appliqué

1. Center an I piece on a white Y. Pin 4 Fs and 4 Gs in place on each spoke of I stem (Four-Tulip Diagram). Tuck 4 Ds under tulips. When satisfied with placement, appliqué pieces in place. Make 5 four-tulip blocks.

2. Lay out partial rings, four-tulip blocks, remaining Ys, and 4 Z triangles (Quilt Assembly Diagram). Starting at center, join rings to adjacent Ys to form circles as

continued

Quilt Assembly Diagram

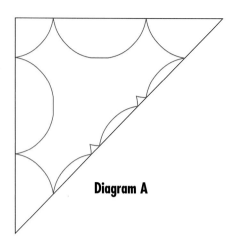

Diagram A

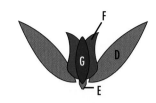

Single Tulip Diagram

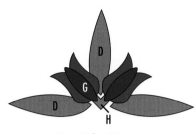

Two-Tulip Diagram

shown, stitching mitered seams to join adjacent rings. Set in 8 A pieces to outside edge of center unit as shown.

3. Join outer segments surrounding each Z triangle. Appliqué edges of surrounding arcs to each Z triangle (Diagram A).

Borders

1. Layer 2 white border strips, right sides facing (Diagram B). Use an acrylic ruler to measure a 45° angle, and mark sewing line from corner to edge of strips. Stitch through both strips on marked line. Trim excess fabric as shown. Repeat with second pair of strips. Press seam allowances to one side or open, as desired (Diagram C).
2. Layer both sections, right sides facing (Diagram D). Stitch 45°-angle seams as before.

3. Unfold window border and press (Diagram E).
4. Center pieced quilt over window border. Appliqué outer edges of circle segments to white border. (Y template can be used as a guide here.)
5. Pin 1 each of E, F, and G at each mitered corner seam. Tuck Ds under tulip as shown (Single Tulip Diagram). Then pin 4 two-tulip units on each outside edge (Two-Tulip Diagram). When satisfied with placement, appliqué each tulip section in place.
6. When appliqué is complete, carefully trim excess white fabric from behind rings, leaving at least ¼" seam allowance.
7. Center a green border strip on each edge and stitch borders to quilt, mitering corners.

Quilting and Finishing

1. Mark quilt top with desired quilting designs. On quilt shown, Elsie quilted cross-hatching behind quilted feather plumes, hearts, and love birds, which are trapuntoed for added dimension. Design your own quilting motifs or look for commercial stencil designs that will fit these areas.
2. Layer backing, batting, and quilt top. Baste. Quilt as desired.
3. Join 1"-wide white strips end-to-end in a continuous strip. Fold strip over cording, wrong sides facing and raw edges together. Use a zipper foot (or equivalent) to stitch close to cording. With raw edges aligned, baste piping to outer edge of quilt.
4. Make 10 yards of continuous bias or straight-grain binding Bind quilt edges.

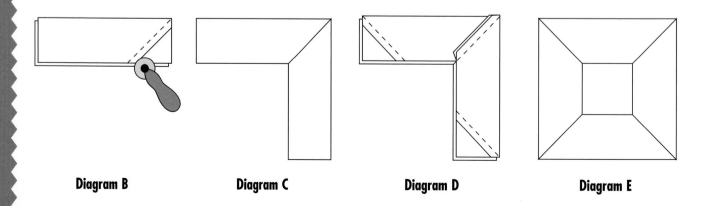

Diagram B   **Diagram C**   **Diagram D**   **Diagram E**

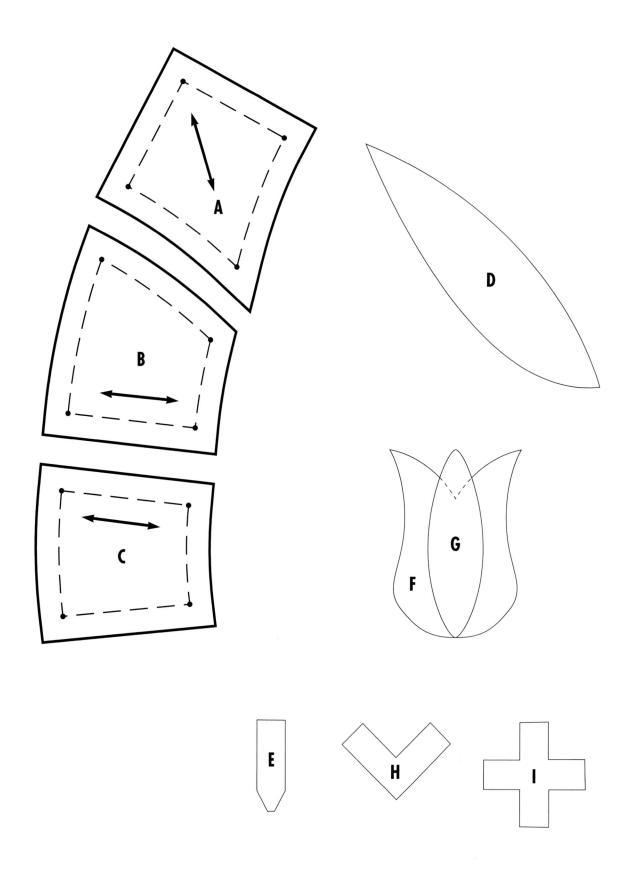

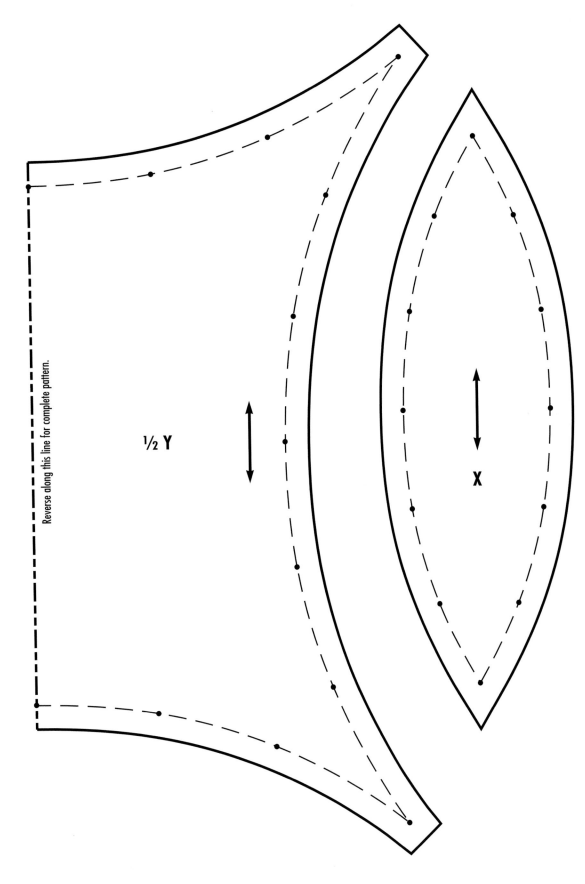

Reverse along this line for complete pattern.

½ Y

X

MILKY WAY

Quilt by Mary Radke of Yorkville, Illinois

Tessellating patterns like this one are fun and interesting to sew. Tessellated means tiled, or interlocking. Though you see a galaxy of stars in the finished quilt, there is no star block—the stars appear only after you join units together.

Finished Size
Quilt: 28" x 28"

Materials
6 (1½" x 21") strips light plaids
9 (2⅞" x 21") strips light plaids
3 (1½" x 21") strips gold plaid
3 (1½" x 21") strips olive plaid
10 (2⅞" x 21") strips medium and dark plaids
4 (1½" x 42") strips dark plaid for inner borders
¼ yard binding fabric
1 yard backing fabric

Cutting
Cut pieces in order listed to get best use of yardage.
From 2⅞"-wide light strips
• 54 (2⅞") squares. Cut squares in half diagonally to get 108 triangles.
• 12 (2½") squares for light star centers.
From medium and dark strips
• 54 (2⅞") squares. Cut squares in half diagonally to get 108 triangles.
• 17 (2½") squares.

Four-Patch Diagram

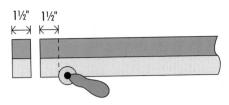

Strip Set Diagram

Four-Patch Assembly

1. Join 1½"-wide light plaid strips and gold strips in pairs to make 3 strip sets (Strip Set Diagram). Make 3 more strip sets with olive fabric. Press seam allowances toward dark fabrics.
2. From each strip set, cut 12 (1½"-wide) segments.
3. Join matching segments to make 36 four-patch units (Four-Patch Diagram).

Quilt Assembly

1. Join light and dark triangles in pairs to make 108 triangle-squares. Press seam allowances toward darker fabrics.
2. Lay out four-patch units, triangle-squares, and 2½" squares in 11 rows as shown (Row Assembly Diagram). Match 4 triangle-square units with same dark color to form stars when rows are joined.
3. Join units in each row. Press seam allowances in opposite directions from row to row. Join rows.

Borders

1. Trim 2 (1½"-wide) border strips to match quilt length. Join strips to quilt sides. Press seam allowances toward borders.
2. Trim remaining border strips to match quilt width. Sew strips to top and bottom edges of quilt.

3. For outer borders, join triangle-squares in 4 rows with 12 units in each row. Join 2 rows to quilt sides. Press seam allowances toward inner border.
4. Join remaining 2½" medium/dark squares to ends of remaining borders. Join these to top and bottom edges of quilt.

Quilting and Finishing

1. Mark quilt top with desired quilting design. Quilt shown was hand-quilted in a diagonal grid.
2. Layer backing, batting, and quilt top. Baste. Quilt as desired.
3. Make 3½ yards of straight-grain binding. Bind quilt edges.

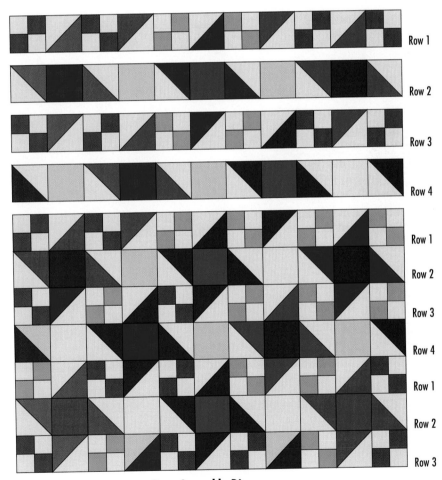

Row Assembly Diagram

STARS WITH FLAIRE

Quilt by Christine Kennedy of Oak Ridge, Tennessee

Bias appliqué around the points of these stars gives this quilt an unusual flair, so Christine Kennedy named her original design *Stars with Flaire*. The colors in the floral fabric set the tone for a coordinating background fabric and scraps. Christine hand-pieced her award-winning quilt, but we offer the option of quick piecing. Patterns for Christine's beautiful quilting designs are on pages 127 and 128.

Finished Size
Quilt: 78" x 95"
Blocks: 20 (17" x 17")

Materials
27 (⅛-yard) pieces coordinating scrap fabrics
4½ yards floral print (includes binding)
4 yards pale pink tone-on-tone print
5¾ yards backing fabric

Cutting
Instructions are for rotary cutting and quick piecing. Cut all strips cross-grain except border strips as noted. For traditional cutting and piecing, use patterns on pages 127 and 128. Cut pieces in order listed to get best use of yardage.

Star Block—Make 20.

From each *scrap fabric*
- 3 (1⅜"-wide) strips to get a total of 80 strips for strip sets (and 1 extra). Divide these into 20 sets (1 for each star block), selecting 4 coordinating strips for set.

From floral print
- 4 (1½" x 94") inner border strips.
- 3 (31") squares for bias appliqué.
- 1 (31") square for binding.
- 23 (1⅜"-wide) strips. From these and narrow length left from previous cuts, cut 100 (1⅜" x 14½") strips for strip sets.

From pink
- 1 (2¾-yard) length. From this, cut 2 (4½" x 99") lengthwise strips for side outer borders and 2 (4½" x 84") strips for top and bottom outer borders. Use leftover from this piece for next 2 steps.
- 20 (8⅜") squares. Cut each square in quarters diagonally to get 80 C triangles.
- 80 (5½") B squares.

Block Assembly

1. For each star, select 1 set of scrap strips and 5 strips of floral print. Floral print is Fabric 1 throughout (see Strip Set Diagrams). Designate each scrap fabric as fabric 2, 3, 4, or 5. From *each* scrap strip, cut 3 (1⅜" x 14½") strips for strip sets.
2. Select 2 floral print strips and 1 each of fabrics 2 and 3. Starting with floral print, join strips as shown (Strip Set 1 Diagram). Instead of matching ends of each new strip, offset each strip about 1½" (this allows you to get more cuts per strip set, reducing waste).
3. Make 1 each of strips sets 2, 3, and 4 in same manner, positioning scrap fabrics consistently as shown. Press seam allowances in strip sets 1 and 3 toward bottom strip and seam allowances in sets 2 and 4 toward top strip.
4. Lay Strip Set 1 on cutting mat with uneven end to your right (if you're left-handed, reverse directions throughout). Position acrylic ruler over strip set, aligning a 45°-angle line with bottom edge of strip set (Diagram A). Trim uneven ends as shown.
5. Turn strip set upside down to continue cutting (Diagram B). Measuring from cut edge, measure 8 (1⅜"-wide) diagonal segments, 1 for each star point. Cut all strip sets in same manner. You should have 1 Fabric 5 strip left over.
6. For each star point, select 1 segment from each strip set. Join these in numerical order (Diagram C), offsetting adjacent segments to match seams correctly. Make 8 diamond-shaped star points.

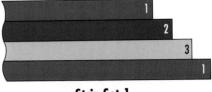

Strip Set 1

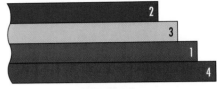

Strip Set 2

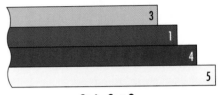

Strip Set 3

Strip Set 4

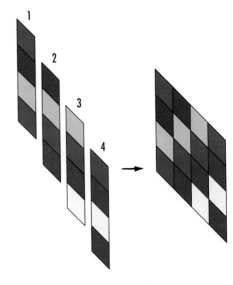

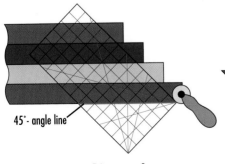

45°- angle line

Diagram A

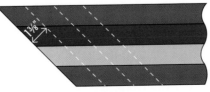

1⅜"

Diagram B

Diagram C

Block Assembly Diagram

7. Join 4 pairs of diamonds, matching seam lines carefully (Block Assembly Diagram). To allow for set-in Bs and Cs, be sure to leave ¼" unstitched at beginning and end of each seam. Join pairs in same manner to make 2 half-star units. Join halves to complete star.

8. Cut 31" floral print square in half diagonally (Photo A). Measuring from cut edges, cut 1"-wide bias strips. Cut these down to 7" lengths. You need 16 (7") bias strips for each block (a total of 320). Fold under ¼" on both long edges of each strip and press. (Set aside remainder for border.)

9. Lightly trace bias placement lines (on patterns B and C) on 4 B squares and 4 C triangles. Appliqué bias strips in place, trimming ends of bias even with edges of each piece.

10. Set-in Bs and Cs as shown to complete each block, sewing bias ends into each seam (Block Assembly Diagram). Make 20 blocks.

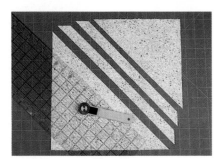

Photo A

Quilt Assembly

1. Lay out blocks in 5 horizontal rows with 4 blocks in each row. When satisfied with block placement, join blocks in each row.
2. Join rows.

Borders

1. From remainder of floral print bias fabric, cut 72 (7"-long) bias strips.
2. Trace bias placement lines from Border Quilting Pattern to each pink border strip, leaving at least 2" of extra fabric at ends of each border strip. Appliqué 20 bias strips on each of 2 side borders and 16 bias strips each on top and bottom borders, trimming ends of bias even with border edges.
3. Matching centers, stitch an inner border strip to bottom edge of each pink border strip.
4. Matching centers of border strips with middle point of each side, sew borders to each side of quilt and miter corners.

Quilting and Finishing

1. Mark quilt top with desired quilting patterns. Patterns for quilting designs in B squares, C triangles, and outer border are on pages 127 and 128.

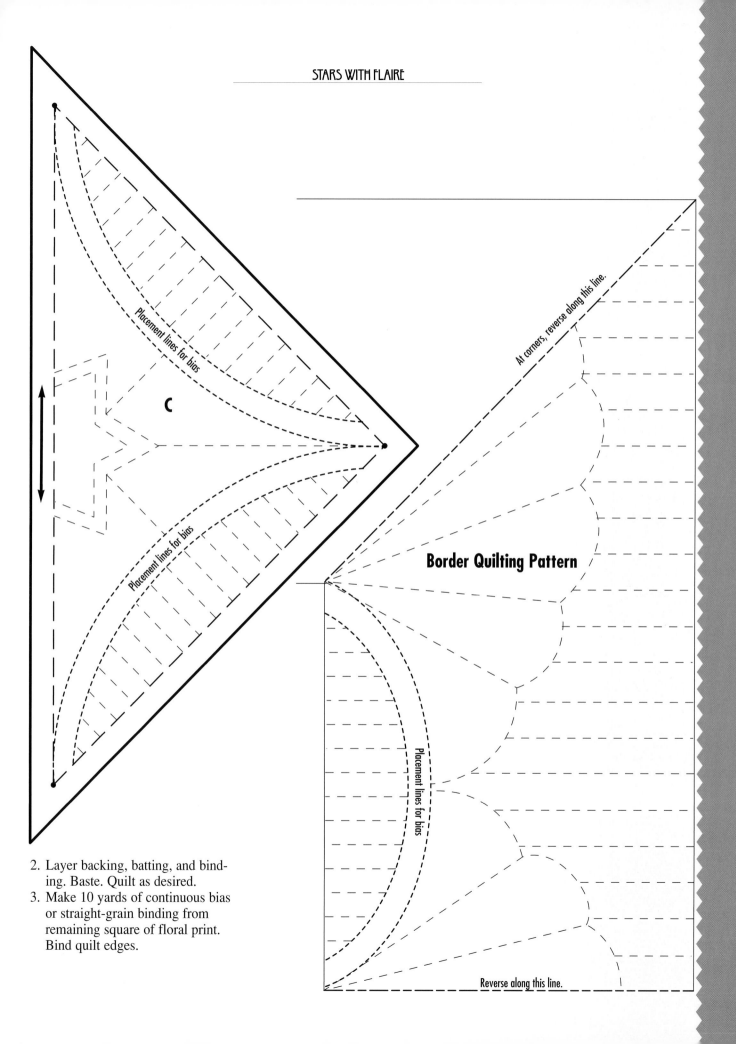

C

Placement lines for bias

Placement lines for bias

At corners, reverse along this line.

Border Quilting Pattern

Placement lines for bias

Reverse along this line.

2. Layer backing, batting, and binding. Baste. Quilt as desired.

3. Make 10 yards of continuous bias or straight-grain binding from remaining square of floral print. Bind quilt edges.

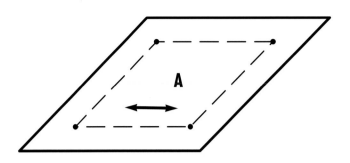

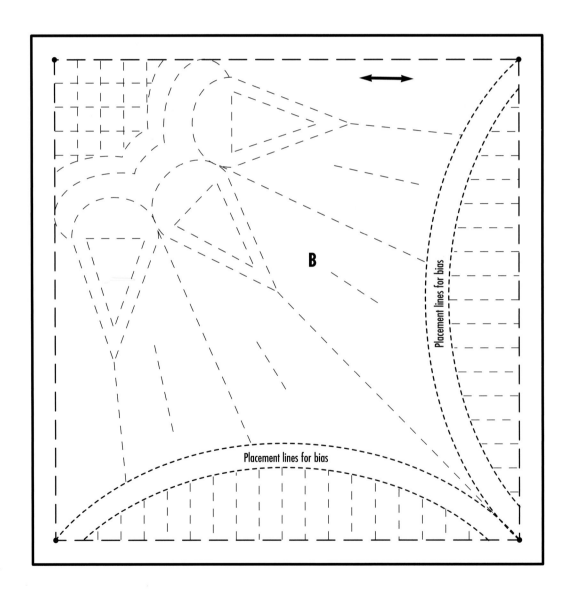

Placement lines for bias

Placement lines for bias

RE-VISION

ew of us are lucky enough to
have the number of reproduction
fabrics that Linda Anderson owns.
She won this collection of fabrics at
a quilt show. This quilt is Linda's
interpretation of the many scrap
quilts her grandmother made for
Lutheran missions. There are nearly
100 fabrics in Linda's quilt—our
instructions call for 25, which is in
keeping with most people's scrap
bag and still gives plenty of variety.

Finished Size

Quilt: 83" x 83"
Blocks: 41 (9" x 9")

Materials

¼ yard *each* of 25 print fabrics
5½ yards white or muslin
2½ yards 90"-wide backing fabric
continued

Quilt by Linda Anderson of Fresno, California

Cutting

Instructions are for rotary cutting and quick piecing. Cut all strips cross-grain except border strips as noted. Cut pieces in order listed to get best use of yardage.

From each scrap fabric
- 2 (1½"-wide) strips. From these, cut 5 (1½" x 8") pieces for strip sets 1 and 2, 3 (1½" x 11") pieces for Strip Set 4, and 5 (1½" x 2½") F pieces.
- 1 (3½"-wide) strip. From this, cut 1 (3½" x 13") piece for Strip Set 3, 9 (3") squares for prairie points, and 2 (1½" x 2½") F pieces. Seven F pieces are extras.

From all remaining scrap fabrics
- 1 (1½"-wide) strip from each of 9 fabrics. From each of these, cut 3 (1½" x 11") pieces for Strip Set 4.
- 4 (2⅜") squares from each of 4 fabrics. Cut each square in half diagonally to get 8 Z triangles of each fabric for Pinwheel blocks.

From white
- 1 (2⅜-yard) length. From this, cut 4 (6" x 85") lengthwise strips for borders. From remainder, cut 100 (1½" x 8") pieces for strip sets 1 and 2.
- 9 (3½"-wide) strips. From these, cut 100 (3½") B squares.
- 2 (5½"-wide) strips. From these, cut 16 (5½") C squares.
- 25 (1½"-wide) strips. From these, cut 32 (1½" x 10½") G strips, 32 (1½" x 9½") E strips, 32 (1½" x 7½") D strips, and 4 (1½" x 12½") H strips.
- 4 (11") squares. Cut each square in quarters diagonally to get 16 X setting triangles.
- 2 (7⅜") squares. Cut each square in half diagonally to get 4 Y corner triangles.

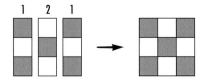

Diagram A

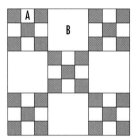

Block 1—Make 25.

Block 1 Assembly

1. Stitch a 1½" x 8" white strip between 2 strips of same print fabric to make Strip Set 1 (Strip Set 1 Diagram). Make 2 of Strip Set 1. Then stitch 1 strip of same print fabric between 2 white strips to make 1 of Strip Set 2 (Strip Set 2 Diagram). Press all seam allowances toward print fabric.
2. Cut 5 (1½"-wide) segments from each strip set.
3. Join 2 segments of Strip Set 1 and 1 segment of Strip Set 2 to make a nine-patch unit (Diagram A). Using all cut segments, you can make 5 nine-patch units of same fabric combination.
4. Repeat with remaining 1½" x 8" strips to get a total of 125 nine-patch units.
5. For each block, select 5 assorted nine-patches and 4 B squares. Join squares in horizontal rows (Block Diagram); then join rows to complete block.
6. Make 25 of Block 1.

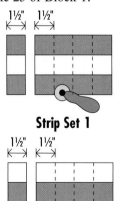

1½" 1½"

Strip Set 1

1½" 1½"

Strip Set 2

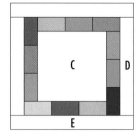

Block 2—Make 16.

Block 2 Assembly

1. Join any 3 (3½" x 13") strips (Strip Set 3 Diagram). Make 8 of Strip Set 3, varying fabrics. You will have 1 (3½" x 13") strip left over.
2. From each strip set, cut 8 (1½"-wide) segments to get a total of 64 segments, 4 for each block.
3. Match 1 segment to a C square, right sides facing and aligning top of segment with corner of square. Stitch segment to square, stopping at least 2" from corner of square, leaving end of segment unsewn (Diagram B). Press seam allowances toward colored strip.
4. Sew second segment to top edge of combined units as shown. Press seam allowances toward print fabrics. Add third and fourth segments in same manner. Then go back and finish first seam, stitching over last segment.

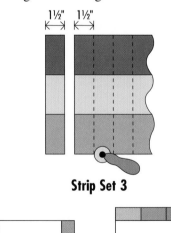

1½" 1½"

Strip Set 3

C

Diagram B

5. Sew D strips to 2 sides of block. Press seam allowances toward Ds. Then stitch E strips to remaining sides to complete block.

6. Make 16 of Block 2.

Side & Corner Blocks Assembly

1. For each side block, select 1 X triangle, 9 F pieces, and 2 Gs. Join 4 Fs in a row; then stitch row to 1 side of triangle (Side Block Diagram). Press seam allowances toward

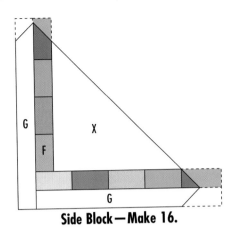

Side Block—Make 16.

pieced row. Join remaining 5 Fs in a row and stitch row to second side of triangle. Last brick in each row extends past triangle; these are trimmed later.

2. Sew 1 G strip to triangle side as shown. Press seam allowance toward pieced row. Stitch second G to adjacent triangle side in same manner to complete block.

3. Make 16 side blocks.

continued

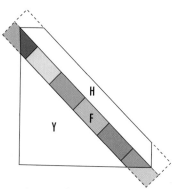

Corner Block—Make 4.

4. For each corner block, select 1 Y triangle, 6 F pieces, and 1 H strip. Join Fs in a row (Corner Block Diagram); then sew row to diagonal edge of triangle. Handle triangle carefully as this edge is bias and can stretch if you're not careful. Join H strip to pieced row. Press seam allowances toward pieced row. Make 4 corner blocks.

Quilt Assembly

1. Lay out blocks in 9 diagonal rows as shown (Quilt Assembly Diagram). Start and end each row with Block 1 and alternate blocks as shown. When satisfied with block placement, join blocks in each row.
2. Add side blocks to row ends as shown.
3. Join rows, mitering seams where side blocks meet.
4. Add corner blocks at each corner of quilt.
5. Trim ends of pieced print strips even with X and Y triangles.

Borders

1. Select 2 (1½" x 11") strips of same print fabric and 1 strip of another fabric. Join strips as shown (Strip Set 4 Diagram). Press all seam allowances toward top strip. Make 34 of Strip Set 4.
2. Cut 4 (2½"-wide) segments from each strip set to get a total of 136 segments for border.
3. Referring to photo, join 34 segments in a vertical row for each side border. Turn adjacent

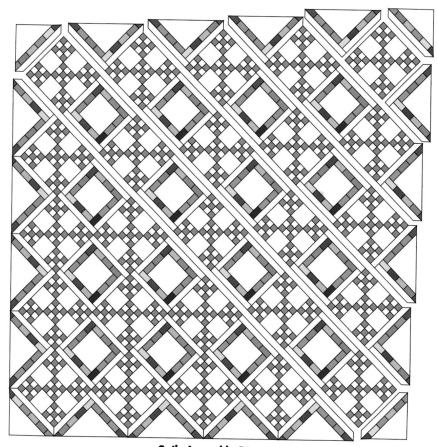

Quilt Assembly Diagram

segments to offset seam allowances. Stitch rows to quilt sides, easing to fit as needed.
4. Join 2 horizontal rows with 34 segments in each row. Set aside.
5. For each Pinwheel block, select 4 Z triangles each of 2 fabrics. Join pairs of contrasting triangles to make 4 triangle-squares. Join squares in rows; then join rows to complete block (Pinwheel Block Diagram). Make 2 Pinwheel blocks with same fabric combination; then make 2 more blocks of second fabric combination.

6. Stitch Pinwheel blocks to both ends of each pieced border. Stitch borders to top and bottom edges of quilt, easing to fit as needed.
7. Measure length of quilt through center of quilt top. Trim 2 white border strips to match length. Stitch border strips to quilt sides. Press seam allowances toward borders.
8. Measure width of quilt through center of quilt top, including side borders. Trim remaining white borders to match quilt width. Sew borders to top and bottom edges of quilt, easing to fit as needed.

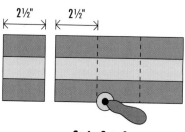

Strip Set 4

Pinwheel Block Diagram

Quilting and Finishing

1. Mark quilt top with desired quilting design. Blocks of quilt shown are machine-quilted in-the-ditch and other areas of quilt are utility-quilted by hand. Pattern for heart-and-wave motif stitched in X triangles is on this page. Same heart is quilted in each B square, and wavy lines in D, E, G, and H strips as well as white border. Linda also added tying in pieced border because her grandmother usually tied her quilts.

2. Layer backing, batting, and quilt top. Baste. Quilt as desired.

3. Fold 56 (3") squares in half (Diagram C) and in half again (Diagram D). Press. Pin prairie points to one side edge of quilt top, aligning raw edges and overlapping points as needed to fit edge of quilt (Diagram E). Baste. Repeat on each remaining side.

4. Fold backing of quilt away from edges; pin or baste to hold backing temporarily in place. Using a ¼" seam, stitch around edges of quilt through prairie points, quilt top, and batting.

5. Trim batting close to stitching. Press prairie points out. Remove pins or basting from backing. Turn under ¼" on each edge of backing and slipstitch backing in place behind prairie points.

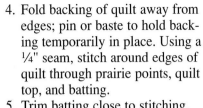

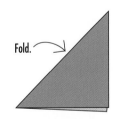

Diagram C

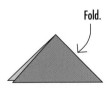

Diagram D   **Diagram E**

Heart-and-Wave Quilting Pattern

WILD GOOSE CHASE

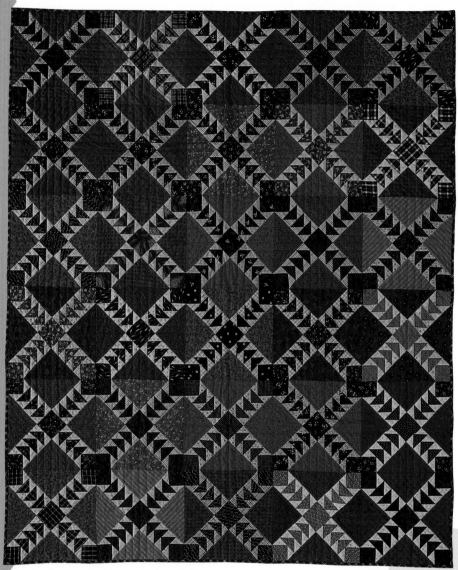

Quilt by Carole Collins of Norfolk, Nebraska

Antique scrap quilts fascinate Carole Collins, who loves making reproductions of her favorite patterns. In pioneer days, fabric was too precious a commodity for quiltmakers to worry whether prints coordinated. Carole's quilt captures that exuberant love of fabric, blending prints, plaids, and stripes in a joyous mix that guarantees satisfaction in any color scheme.

Finished Size
Quilt: 75" x 90"
Blocks: 30 (15" x 15")

Materials
30 (11¼") squares red prints
15 (¼-yard) pieces navy and/or gold prints and plaids
15 (¼-yard) pieces light shirting prints and plaids
⅞ yard binding fabric
5½ yards backing fabric

Cutting
Instructions are for rotary cutting and quick piecing. Cut all strips cross-grain. Cut pieces in order listed to get best use of yardage.
From each *navy/gold print*
• 2 (4"-wide) strips. From these, cut 2 (4") E squares and 24 (2¼" x 4") B pieces.
• 8 (3") D squares.
From each *light shirting print*
• 1 (2⅝"-wide) strip. From this, cut 8 (2⅝") squares. Cut each square in half diagonally to get 16 C triangles.
• 48 (2¼") A squares.

Wild Goose Chase Block — Make 30.

Block Assembly

1. For each block, choose 24 A squares and 8 C triangles of same fabric. Select 12 Bs, 4 D squares, and 1 E of 1 fabric.
2. Match corners of 1 A and 1 B, right sides facing (Diagram A). See page 11 for step-by-step instructions on diagonal-corner quick-piecing technique. Stitch A to B, trim seam allowance, and press A to right side. Stitch another A square to opposite corner of B as shown. Press. Make 12 matching Goose Chase units.
3. Stitch a C triangle to 1 side of a D square (Diagram B). Sew a second C triangle to adjacent side as shown. Press seam allowances toward Cs. Make 4 matching corner units.
4. Join 1 corner unit and 3 Goose Chase units in a row as shown (Diagram C). Make 4 pieced units.
5. Choose 1 red fabric square. Cut square in quarters diagonally to get 4 F triangles. Join F triangles to both sides of 2 pieced rows (Block Assembly Diagram). Press seam allowances toward red.
6. Join remaining pieced rows to opposite sides of E square. Press seam allowances toward E.
7. Join triangle units to center pieced row to complete block.
8. Make 30 Wild Goose Chase blocks.

Quilt Assembly

1. Lay out blocks in 6 horizontal rows with 5 blocks in each row. When satisfied with block placement, join blocks in each row.
2. Join rows.

Quilting and Finishing

1. Mark quilt top with desired quilting design. Quilt shown is quilted in-the-ditch around each goose, and red triangles are quilted in parallel lines.
2. Layer backing, batting, and quilt top. Baste. Quilt as desired.
3. Make 9⅜ yards of continuous bias or straight-grain binding. Bind quilt edges.

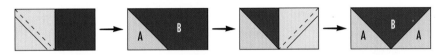

Diagram A

Diagram B

Diagram C

Block Assembly Diagram

STAR QUILT

Quilt by Linda Gibson of Cumming, Iowa

This star block is not an old pattern, but Linda Gibson gave it the look of an antique with her choice of subdued colors and fabric prints. If you can't figure out where the block is in this quilt, here's a hint—the dark stars are formed by the block corners.

Finished Size
Quilt: 91" x 104"
Blocks: 42 (13" x 13")

Materials
8 (1-yard) pieces beige prints
14 (¼-yard) pieces light-colored prints
14 (¼-yard) pieces medium-colored prints
20 (⅜-yard) pieces very dark prints
8¼ yards backing fabric

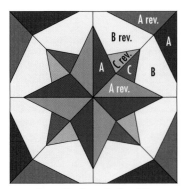

Star Block—Make 42.

Cutting

Cut all strips cross-grain. Make templates of patterns A, B, C, and D on page 139. Cut pieces in order listed to get best use of yardage.

From beige prints
- 21 (8"-wide) strips. From these, cut 168 of Pattern B and 168 of Pattern B reversed. Set aside 42 matched sets of 8 (4 B, 4 B rev.) for blocks.
- 56 of Pattern D for border units.

From each light-colored print
- 3 (2½"-wide) strips. From these, cut 168 of Pattern A and 168 of Pattern C. Set aside 42 matched sets of 4 for blocks.

From each medium-colored print
- 3 (2½"-wide) strips. From these, cut 168 of Pattern A reversed and 168 of Pattern C reversed. Set aside 42 matched sets of 4.

From very dark prints
- 27 (6½"-wide) strips. From these, cut 224 of Pattern A and 224 of Pattern A reversed.
- 224 (4") squares for prairie points.

Block Assembly

1. For each block, select matched sets of 4 light print A pieces and 4 medium print A reversed pieces for center star. Then choose a matched set of 4 Bs and 4 Bs reversed for beige background, and matched sets of 4 Cs and 4 Cs reversed for small star points. Finally, choose 4 dark A pieces and 4 dark A reversed pieces, mixing fabrics as desired.

2. Sew each C piece to a B and each C reversed to a B reversed as shown (Block Assembly Diagram). Press seam allowances toward Bs. Then add A and A reversed pieces to each unit to get 8 triangular sections. Press seam allowances toward As.

3. Join 2 sections as shown to get 4 square quadrants. Join quadrants to complete block.

4. Make 42 star blocks.

5. For each border block, select 1 dark A, 1 dark A reversed, and 1 D piece. Stitch each A piece to edge of D as shown (Diagram A); then stitch mitered seam to join A pieces. Make 56 border blocks.

continued

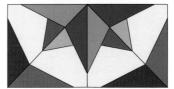

Block Assembly Diagram

Diagram A

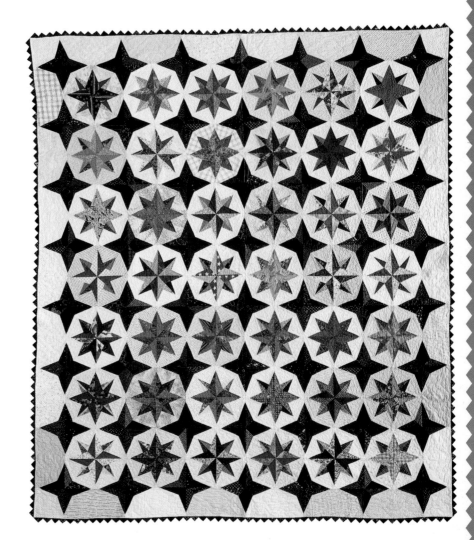

Quilt Assembly

1. Lay out star blocks in 7 horizontal rows with 6 blocks in each row (Quilt Assembly Diagram). Add 2 border blocks with Ds adjacent at ends of each row as shown.
2. For top border row, lay out 14 border blocks, rotating as shown. Repeat for bottom border row.
3. Arrange blocks to get a pleasing balance of color and value. When satisfied with block placement, join blocks in each row.
4. Join rows.

Quilting and Finishing

1. Mark quilt top with desired quilting design. On quilt shown, A and C pieces are quilted in-the-ditch; dark stars are quilted ⅜" and 1" inside seam lines with contrasting thread. Designs quilted in B and D pieces are shown on patterns.
2. Layer backing, batting, and quilt top. Baste. Quilt as desired.
3. Fold 59 dark squares in half (Diagram B) and in half again (Diagram C). Press. Pin prairie points to 1 side edge of quilt top, aligning raw edges and overlapping points as needed to fit edge of quilt (Diagram D). Baste. Repeat on opposite side.
4. Fold, press, and pin 53 prairie points in same manner for each top and bottom border.
5. Fold backing of quilt away from edges; pin or baste to hold backing temporarily in place. Using a ¼" seam, stitch around edges of quilt through prairie points, quilt top, and batting.
6. Trim batting close to stitching. Press prairie points out. Remove pins or basting from backing. Turn under ¼" on each edge of backing and slipstitch backing in place behind prairie points.

Quilt Assembly Diagram

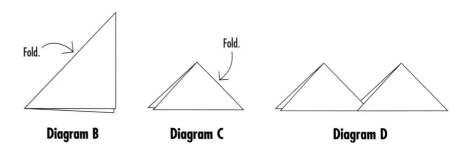

Diagram B   **Diagram C**   **Diagram D**

Fold.   Fold.

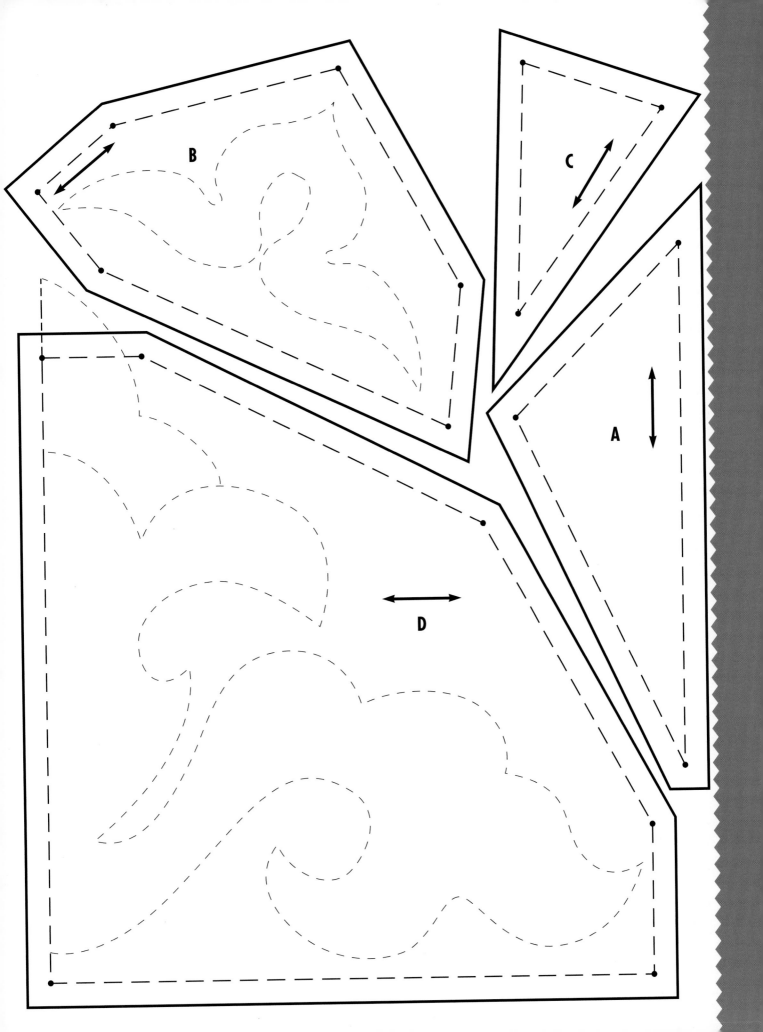

B

C

A

D

QUILT SMART WORKSHOP
A Guide to Basic Quiltmaking

Preparing Fabric

Before cutting any pieces, be sure to wash and dry your fabric to preshrink it. All-cotton fabrics may need pressing before cutting. Trim selvages from the fabric before you cut pieces.

Making Templates

Before you can make one of the quilts in this book, you must make templates from the printed patterns given. (Not all pieces require patterns—some pieces are meant to be cut with a rotary cutter and ruler.) Quilters have used many materials to make templates, including cardboard and sandpaper. Transparent template plastic, available at craft supply and quilt shops, is durable, see-through, and easy to use.

To make a plastic template, place the plastic sheet on the printed page and use a laundry marker or permanent fine-tip marking pen to trace each pattern. For machine piecing, trace on the outside solid (cutting) line. For hand piecing, trace on the inside broken (stitching) line. Cut out the template on the traced line. Label each template with the pattern name, letter, grain line arrow, and match points (corner dots).

Marking and Cutting Fabric for Piecing

Place the template facedown on the wrong side of the fabric and mark around it with a sharp pencil.

If you will be piecing by machine, the pencil lines represent cutting lines. Cut on each marked line.

For hand piecing, the pencil lines are seam lines. Leave at least ¾" between marked lines for seam allowances. Add ¼" seam allowance around each piece as you cut. Mark match points (corner dots) on each piece.

You can do without templates if you use a rotary cutter and ruler to cut straight strips and geometric shapes such as squares and triangles. Rotary cutting is always paired with machine piecing, and pieces are cut with seam allowances included.

Hand Piecing

To hand piece, place two fabric pieces together with right sides facing. Insert a pin in each match point of the top piece. Stick the pin through both pieces and check to be sure that it pierces the match point on the bottom piece (Figure 1). Adjust the pieces as necessary to align the match points. (The raw edges of the

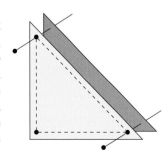

Figure 1—Aligning Match Points

two pieces may not align exactly.) Pin the pieces securely together.

Sew with a running stitch of 8 to 10 stitches per inch. Sew from match point to match point, checking the stitching as you go to be sure you are sewing in the seam line of both pieces.

To make sharp corners, begin and end the stitching exactly at the match point; do not stitch into the seam allowances. When joining units where several seams come together, do not sew over seam allowances; sew through them at the point where all seam lines meet (Figure 2).

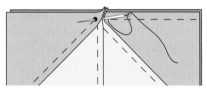

Figure 2—Pressing Intersecting Seams

Always press both seam allowances to one side. Pressing the seam open, as in dressmaking, can leave gaps between stitches through which the batting may beard. Press seam allowances toward the darker fabric whenever you can, but it is sometimes more important to reduce bulk by avoiding overlapping seam allowances. When four or more seams meet at one point, such as at the corner of a block, press all the seams in a "swirl" in the same direction to reduce bulk (Figure 3).

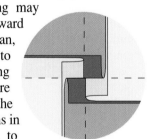

Figure 3—Joining Units

Machine Piecing

To machine piece, place two fabric pieces together with right sides facing. Align match points as described under "Hand Piecing" and pin the pieces together securely.

Set the stitch length at 12 to 15 stitches per inch. At this setting, you do not need to backstitch to lock seam beginnings and ends. Use a presser foot that gives a perfect ¼" seam allowance, or measure ¼" from the needle and mark that point on the presser foot with nail polish or masking tape.

Chain piecing, stitching edge to edge, saves time when sewing similar sets of pieces (Figure 4). Join the first two

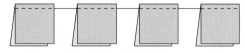

Figure 4—Chain Piecing

pieces as usual. At the end of the seam, do not backstitch, cut the thread, or lift the presser foot. Instead, sew a few stitches off the fabric. Place the next two pieces and continue stitching. Keep sewing until all the sets are joined. Then cut the sets apart.

Press the seam allowances toward the darker fabric whenever possible. When you join blocks or rows, press the seam allowances of the top row in one direction and the seam allowances of the bottom row in the opposite direction to help ensure that the seams will lie flat (Figure 5).

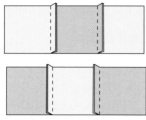

Figure 5—Pressing Seams for Machine Piecing

Hand Appliqué

Hand appliqué is the best way to achieve the look of traditional appliqué. However, using freezer paper, which is sold in grocery stores, saves a lot of time because it eliminates the need for hand basting the seam allowances.

Make templates without seam allowances. Trace the template onto the dull side of the freezer paper and cut the paper on the marked line. Make a freezer-paper shape for each piece to be appliquéd.

Pin the freezer-paper shape, shiny side up, to the wrong side of the fabric. Following the paper shape and adding a scant ¼" seam allowance, cut out the fabric piece. Do not remove the pins. Use the tip of a hot, dry iron to press the seam allowance to the shiny side of the freezer paper. Be careful not to touch the shiny side of the freezer paper with the iron. Remove the pins.

Pin the appliqué shape in place on the background fabric. Use one strand of sewing thread in a color to match the appliqué shape. Using a very small slipstitch (Figure 6) or blindstitch (Figure 7), appliqué the shape to the background fabric.

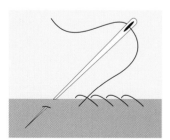

Figure 6—Slipstitch

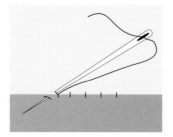

Figure 7—Blindstitch

When your stitching is complete, cut away the background fabric behind the appliqué, leaving ¼" seam allowance. Separate the freezer paper from the fabric with your fingernail and pull gently to remove it.

Mitering Borders

Mitered borders require a little extra care to stitch but offer a very nice finish when square (butted) border corners just won't do.

First, measure the length of the quilt through the middle of the quilt top. Cut two border strips to fit this length, plus the width of the border plus 2". Centering the measurement on the strip, place pins on the edge of each strip at the center and each end of the measurement. Match the pins on each border strip to the corners of a long side of the quilt. Starting and stopping ¼" from each corner of the quilt, sew the borders to the quilt, easing the quilt to fit between the pins (Figure 8). Press the seam allowances toward border strip.

Measure the quilt width through the middle and cut two border strips to fit, adding the border width plus 2". Join these borders to opposite ends of the quilt in the same manner.

Fold one border corner over adjacent corner as shown (Figure 9) and press. On wrong side, stitch in the creased fold to complete the mitered seam (Figure 10). Press; then check to make sure corner lies flat on quilt top. Trim seam allowances.

Figure 8

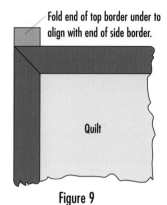

Fold end of top border under to align with end of side border.

Figure 9

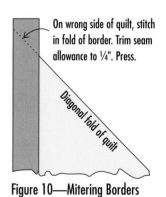

On wrong side of quilt, stitch in fold of border. Trim seam allowance to ¼". Press.

Diagonal fold of quilt

Figure 10—Mitering Borders

Marking Your Quilt Top

When the quilt top is complete, press it thoroughly before marking it with quilting designs. The most popular methods for marking use stencils or templates. Both can be purchased, or you can make your own. You can use a yardstick to mark straight lines or grids.

Use a silver quilter's pencil for marking light to medium fabrics and a white chalk pencil on dark fabrics. Lightly mark the quilt top with your chosen quilting designs.

Making a Backing

The instructions in this book give backing yardage based on 45"-wide fabric unless a 90"-wide or 108"-wide backing is more practical. (These wide fabrics are sold at fabric and quilt shops.) Pieced or not, the quilt backing should be at least 3" larger on all sides than the quilt top.

Backing fabric should be of a type and color that is compatible with the quilt top. Percale sheets are not recommended, because they are tightly woven and difficult to hand-quilt through.

A pieced backing for a bed quilt should have three panels. The three-panel backing is recommended because it tends to wear better and lie flatter than the two-panel type, the center seam of which often makes a ridge down the center of the quilt. Begin by cutting the fabric in half widthwise (Figure 11). Open the two lengths and stack them, with right sides facing and selvages aligned. Stitch along both selvage edges to create a tube of fabric (Figure 12). Cut down the center of the top layer of fabric only and open the fabric flat (Figure 13). Press seam allowances toward center panel.

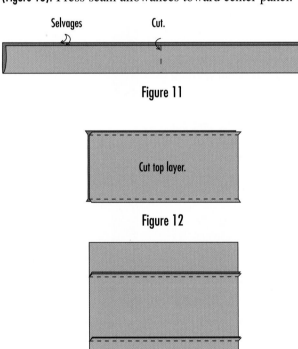

Figure 11

Figure 12

Figure 13

Layering and Basting

Prepare a working surface to spread out the quilt. Place the backing on the surface, right side down. Unfold the batting and place it on top of the backing. Smooth any wrinkles or lumps in the batting. Lay the quilt top right side up on top of the batting and backing. Make sure backing and quilt top are parallel.

Use a darning needle for basting, with a long strand of sewing thread. Begin in the center of your quilt and baste out toward the edges. The stitches should cover enough of the quilt to keep the layers from shifting during quilting. Inadequate basting can result in puckers and folds on the back and front of the quilt during quilting.

Hand Quilting

Hand quilting can be done with the quilt in a hoop or in a floor frame. It is best to start in the middle of your quilt and quilt out toward the edges.

Most quilters use a thin, short needle called a "between." Betweens are available in sizes 7 to 12, with 7 being the longest and 12 the shortest. If you are a beginning quilter, try a size 7 or 8. Because betweens are so much shorter than other needles, they may feel awkward at first. As your skill increases, try using a smaller needle to help you make smaller stitches.

Quilting thread, heavier and stronger than sewing thread, is available in a wide variety of colors. If color matching is critical and you can't find the color you need, you can substitute cotton sewing thread if you coat it with beeswax before quilting to prevent it from tangling.

Thread your needle with a 20" length and make a small knot at one end. Insert the needle into the quilt top approximately ½" from the point where you want to begin quilting. Do not take the needle through all three layers, but stop it in the batting and bring it up through the quilt top again at your starting point. Tug gently on the thread to pop the knot through the quilt top into the batting. This anchors the thread without an unsightly knot showing on the back.

With your non-sewing hand underneath the quilt, insert the needle with the point straight down in the quilt about ¹⁄₁₆" from the starting point. With your underneath finger, feel for the point as the needle comes through the backing (Figure 14). Place the thumb of your sewing hand about ½" ahead of the needle. When you feel the needle touch your underneath finger, push the fabric up from below as you rock the needle down to a nearly horizontal position. Using

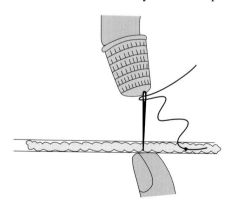

Figure 14—Hand Quilting

the thumb of your sewing hand in conjunction with the underneath hand, pinch a little hill in the fabric and push the tip of the needle back through the quilt top (**Figure 15**).

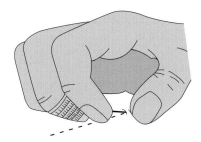

Figure 15—Hand Quilting

Now either push the needle through to complete one stitch or rock the needle again to an upright position on its point to take another stitch. Take no more than a quarter-needleful of stitches before pulling the needle through.

When you have 6" of thread remaining, you must end the old thread securely and invisibly. Carefully tie a knot in the thread, flat against the surface of the fabric. Pop the knot through the top as you did when beginning the line of quilting. Clip the thread, rethread your needle, and continue quilting.

Machine Quilting

Machine quilting is as old as the sewing machine itself; but until recently, it was thought inferior to hand quilting. Fine machine quilting is as beautiful as hand quilting, but it requires a different set of skills from hand quilting.

Machine quilting can be done on your sewing machine using a straight stitch and a special presser foot. A walking foot or even-feed foot is recommended for straight-line quilting to help the top fabric move through the machine at the same rate that the feed dogs move the bottom fabric.

Regular sewing thread or nylon thread can be used for machine quilting. With the quilt top facing you, roll the long edges of the basted quilt toward the center, leaving a 12"-wide area unrolled in the center. Secure the roll with bicycle clips, metal bands that are available at quilt shops. Begin at one unrolled end and fold the quilt over and over until only a small area is showing. This will be the area where you will begin to quilt.

Place the folded portion of the quilt in your lap. Start quilting in the center and work to the right, unfolding and unrolling the quilt as you go. Remove the quilt from the machine, turn it, and reinsert it in the machine to stitch the left side. A table placed behind your sewing machine will help support the quilt as it is stitched.

Curves and circles are most easily made by free-motion machine quilting. Using a darning foot and with the feed dogs down, move the quilt under the needle with your fingertips. Place your hands on the fabric on each side of the foot and run the machine at a steady, medium speed. The length of the stitches is determined by the rate of speed at which you move fabric through the machine. Do not rotate the quilt; rather, move it from side to side as needed. Always stop with the needle down to keep the quilt from shifting.

Making Binding

A continuous bias or straight-grain strip is used to bind quilt edges. Bias binding is especially recommended for quilts with curved edges. Follow these steps to make a continuous bias strip:

1. Start with a square of fabric. Multiply the number of binding inches needed by the cut width of the binding strip (usually 2½"). Use a calculator to find the square root of that number. That's the size of the fabric square needed to make your binding.
2. Cut the square in half diagonally.
3. With right sides facing, join triangles to form a sawtooth as shown (**Figure 16**).
4. Press seam open. Mark off parallel lines the desired width of the binding as shown (**Figure 17**).

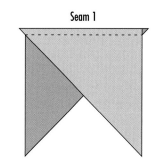

Figure 16—Continuous Bias Binding

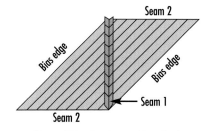

Figure 17—Continuous Bias Binding

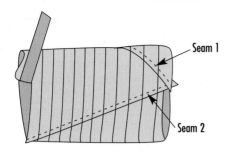

Figure 18—Continuous Bias Binding

5. With right sides facing, align raw edges marked Seam 2. Offset edges by one strip width, so one side is higher than the other **(Figure 18)**. Stitch Seam 2. Press seam open.
6. Cut the binding in a continuous strip, starting with the protruding point and following the marked lines around the tube.
7. Press the binding strip in half lengthwise, with wrong sides facing.

Attaching Binding

To prepare your quilt for binding, baste the layers together ¼" from the edge of the quilt. Trim the backing and batting even with the edge of the quilt top. Beginning at the midpoint of one side of the quilt, pin the binding to the top, with right sides facing and raw edges aligned.

Machine-stitch the binding along one edge of the quilt, sewing through all layers. Backstitch at the beginning of the seam to lock the stitching.

Stitch until you reach the seam line at the corner, and backstitch. Lift the presser foot and turn the quilt to align the foot with the next edge. Continue sewing around all four sides. Join the beginning and end of the binding strip by machine, or stitch one end by hand to overlap the other.

Turn the binding over the edge and blindstitch it in place on the backing. At each corner, fold the excess binding neatly to make a mitered corner and blindstitch it in place.

Making a Hanging Sleeve

Hanging a quilt on a wall adds color and drama to any decor. However, it is important to protect a quilt while showing it off. Only a sturdy, lightweight quilt should be hung. If a quilt is in delicate condition, hanging will only hasten its deterioration.

Do not use pushpins or tacks to hang a quilt because the metal can leave rust stains on the fabric.

The method most often used to hang a quilt is to sew a sleeve on the back so a dowel or slat can be slipped through it. This method distributes the weight evenly across the width of the quilt.

1. From leftover backing fabric, cut an 8"-wide piece that is the same length as the quilt edge. On each end, turn under ½"; then turn under another ½". Topstitch to hem both ends. With wrong sides facing, fold the fabric in half lengthwise and stitch the long edges together. Press seam allowances open and to the middle of the sleeve **(Figure 19)**.

Figure 19—Hanging Sleeve   Figure 20—Hanging Sleeve

2. Center the sleeve on the quilt backing about 1" below the binding with the seam against the backing. Hand-sew the sleeve to the quilt through backing and batting along both long edges. For large quilts, make two or three sleeve sections as shown so you can use more nails or brackets to support the dowel to better distribute the quilt's weight **(Figure 20)**.
3. Screw an eyelet hook into each of the slat or dowel to hang on nails.